I0799164

STUDY GUIDE

Facing the Last Enemy

Death and the Christian

Guy Prentiss Waters

LIGONIER MINISTRIES
Renew your Mind.
LIGONIER.ORG | 800-435-4343

421 Ligonier Court, Sanford, FL 32771
E-mail: info@ligonier.org

Printed in China.

Contents

Introduction

We all have questions about death, but to answer these questions, we need to go to Scripture. There we can find truth about death and dying, truth that we can stake our lives on. In this teaching series, Guy Waters provides sound, practical, and biblical guidance to give us a better grasp on Scripture's testimony about death and dying, which in turn can help us—and help us help others—to face the last enemy.

This study guide is a companion to the video teaching series. Whether you are using the DVDs, streaming the videos on Ligonier.org, or going through the course in Ligonier Connect, this resource is designed to help you make the most of the learning experience. For each message in the series, there is a corresponding lesson in this guide. Here is what you will find in each lesson:

INTRODUCTION	The introduction is a brief paragraph that summarizes the content covered in the lecture and considered in the study guide lesson. **How to use:** Use the introduction to each lesson to get a sense of the big picture before watching the video. Refer to these statements as you work through the study guide to remind yourself of what you have already covered and where you are headed.
LEARNING GOALS	The learning goals are the knowledge and skills that the study guide lesson will endeavor to equip you with as you work through the lecture content. **How to use:** Familiarize yourself with the goals of each lesson before engaging its contents. Keeping the overall purpose in mind as you watch each video and reflect on or discuss the questions will help you get the most out of each lesson.
KEY IDEAS	The key ideas are the major points or takeaways from the lecture. **How to use:** Use these ideas to prepare yourself for each lesson and to review previous lessons. They describe specifically the knowledge that each lecture is communicating.

REFLECTION & DISCUSSION QUESTIONS	The questions are the guided reflection and/or discussion component of the lesson that is intended to help you prepare for, process, and organize what you are learning. **How to use:** Reflect on individually or discuss in a group the questions in the order in which they appear in the lesson. The time stamps in the right margin indicate where the answers to questions during the video can be found.
PRAYER	The prayer section offers suggestions for how to close the lesson in prayer with respect to what was taught in the lecture. **How to use:** Consider using each lesson's prayer section as a guide to personal or group prayer. These sections follow the ACTS prayer model, which you can learn more about in R.C. Sproul's Crucial Questions booklet *Does Prayer Change Things?* This helpful guide is available as a free e-book at Ligonier.org.
REVIEW QUIZ	The review quiz is a set of six multiple-choice questions that appears at the end of each lesson. **How to use:** Use each quiz to check your comprehension and memory of the major points covered in each lecture. It will be most beneficial to your learning if you take a lesson's quiz either sometime between lessons or just before you begin the next lesson in the study guide.
ANSWER KEY	The answer key provides explanations for the reflection and discussion questions and answers to the multiple-choice questions in the review quiz. **How to use:** Use the answer key to check your own answers or when you do not know the answer. Note: Do not give in too quickly; struggling for a few moments to recall an answer reinforces it in your mind.

Study Schedules

The following table suggests four plans for working through the *Facing the Last Enemy* video teaching series and this companion study guide. Whether you are going through this series on your own or with a group, these schedules should help you plan your study path.

	Extended 14-Week Plan	Standard 12-Week Plan	Abbreviated 6-Week Plan	Intensive 4-Week Plan
Week	**Lesson**			
1	*	1	1 & 2	1–3
2	1	2	3 & 4	4–6
3	2	3	5 & 6	7–9
4	3	4	7 & 8	10–12
5	4	5	9 & 10	
6	5	6	11 & 12	
7	6	7		
8	7	8		
9	8	9		
10	9	10		
11	10	11		
12	11	12		
13	12			
14	*			

* For these weeks, rather than completing lessons, spend your time discussing and praying about your learning goals for the study (the first week) and the most valuable takeaways from the study (the last week).

1

What Is Death? Five Foundational Principles

INTRODUCTION

Every human being, at one time or another, has questions about death, but Scripture is the only place where we can turn for good answers to those questions. Apart from Scripture, we cannot even define death. In this lesson, Dr. Waters examines why the subject of death is largely ignored in the world and sometimes even in the church before giving a preliminary sketch of what death is from Genesis 1–3.

LEARNING GOALS

When you have finished this lesson, you should be able to:

- Identify the challenges that Christians face in thinking seriously about death
- Appreciate how the Word of God immediately addresses the sobering reality of death
- Outline five defining features of death as found in Genesis 1–3

KEY IDEAS

- Thinking seriously about death and dying does not come easily to us in the twenty-first century because of developments both inside and outside the church.
- God made a world that is teeming with life with the potential to produce more life, and it was all "very good" (Gen. 1:31).
- Death was not a part of God's very good creation, but death entered the world through sin and is sin's universal and cosmic penalty.

REFLECTION & DISCUSSION QUESTIONS

Before the Video

What Do You Think?

Take a moment to answer the following questions. They will prepare you for the lecture.

- Why are you undertaking this study about death? What do you hope to accomplish?

- What questions or uncertainties do you struggle with the most about death and dying?

Scripture Reading

The LORD God took the man and put him in the garden of Eden to work it and keep it. And the LORD God commanded the man, saying, "You may surely eat of every tree of the garden, but of the tree of the knowledge of good and evil you shall not eat, for in the day that you eat of it you shall surely die." . . . Now the serpent was more crafty than any other beast of the field that the LORD God had made. He said to the woman, "Did God actually say, 'You shall not eat of any tree in the garden'?" And the woman said to the serpent, "We may eat of the fruit of the trees in the garden, but God said, 'You shall not eat of the fruit of the tree that is in the midst of the garden, neither shall you touch it, lest you die.'" But the serpent said to the woman, "You will not surely die."

—Gen. 2:15–17; 3:1–4

- How would you characterize the serpent's manner of tempting Eve?

During the Video

Answer the following questions while you watch the video. They will guide you through the lecture.

Challenges Inside and Out *0:00–10:05*

- How does culture distract and distance us from serious reflection about death?

- How can the church also distract and distance us from serious reflection about death?

Death and Genesis 1–3 *10:05–24:13*

- How does the opening phrase of Genesis, "In the beginning," inform how we understand death?
- How did God make man?
- What are two defining features of death as the penalty for sin?

After the Video

Answer the following questions after you have finished the lecture. They will help you identify and summarize the major points.

- What do you consider to be the most problematic trends in culture and the church that take us away from serious reflection about death and why?

  If you are in a group, have the members discuss what questions about death they hope to have answered by this teaching series and why those questions are important to them.
- Why is it important to affirm that death is the penalty for sin?

  If you are in a group, have the members connect how affirming that death is the penalty for sin helps someone understand what Jesus Christ has done in the gospel.
- Which of the five basic truths about death from Genesis 1–3 stuck out to you the most in driving home the unnaturalness of death or the grievousness of sin?

  If you are in a group, have the members discuss why it is significant that death is so central in the opening chapters of Genesis, yet people attempt to ignore and suppress its reality. Ask: How does God provide an answer to death?

PRAYER

Commit what you have learned from God's Word in this lesson to prayer.

- Praise God for being the one living and true God through whom all things exist.
- Confess ways that you are driven to distraction when it comes to the serious matters of this life.

- Thank God for the truthfulness of His Word concerning the nature of death.
- Ask God to equip you with biblical truth, the encouragement of the Spirit, and confidence in Christ as you continue this study on the last enemy.

REVIEW QUIZ

Use these multiple-choice questions to measure what you learned from this lesson.

1. Which of the following was *not* named as a cultural influence that takes us from away from seriously reflecting on death?
    a. Distance of loved ones at death
    b. Distraction from entertainment
    c. Glorification of violence
    d. New ways of mourning
2. Classic hymns are some of the most popular elements of funerals today.
    a. True
    b. False
3. Which of the following can be understood as paralleling one another in culture and in the church as similar in taking us away from seriously reflecting on death?
    a. Media distraction and worship as entertainment
    b. Distancing experience of the death of loved ones and consumeristic church models
    c. Distancing experience of the death of loved ones and separation in the church
    d. Both a and c
4. When is the first time that death is spoken of in the Bible?
    a. Genesis 1 with the creation of man and woman
    b. Genesis 2 with Adam's call to guard and keep the garden
    c. Genesis 2 with the prohibition of the Tree of Knowledge of Good and Evil
    d. Genesis 3 with Adam's eating the forbidden fruit and being questioned by God
5. Genesis teaches us that death cannot be explained away as natural.
    a. True
    b. False
6. Which of the following passages was connected to the cosmic nature of death?
    a. "For all have sinned and fall short of the glory of God" (Rom. 3:23).
    b. "Sin came into the world through one man" (Rom. 5:12).
    c. "The wages of sin is death" (Rom. 6:23).
    d. "The whole creation has been groaning" (Rom. 8:22).

Answer Key—What Is Death? Five Foundational Principles

REFLECTION & DISCUSSION QUESTIONS

Before the Video

What Do You Think?

These are personal questions. The answers should be based on your own knowledge and experience.

Scripture Reading

- How would you characterize the serpent's manner of tempting Eve?

  God plainly told Adam not to eat from the Tree of Knowledge of Good and Evil, or else death would result. The serpent's speech is not plain but deceptive, intentionally twisting God's words to suggest that He had restricted all the trees of the garden for food. Moving beyond suggestive deception, the serpent outright lies and contradicts what God had said when telling Eve, "You will not surely die."

During the Video

Challenges Inside and Out

- How does culture distract and distance us from serious reflection about death?

  In terms of popular culture, the amount of entertainment on offer indicates that we live in a culture of distraction. The thought of death can seem unbearable, so rather than learning to reflect on it, we are trained to distract ourselves from it. Society in general distances us from death as well. Relatively few young people have direct experience with death because, unlike in years past, many elderly family members die away from the home.

- How can the church also distract and distance us from serious reflection about death?

  Along with the culture, the church can also distract and distance us from the reality of death. The church has at times treated attendees like consumers, and this has contributed to a consumer mentality among attendees, so churches are reluctant to bring up grim realities such as death, lest the "consumer" take his or her business somewhere else. Some churches have also embraced entertainment-based worship, which parallels our culture of distraction, and the way that churches separate people by ages and stages of life means that younger Christians do not feel the weight of death in a congregation or learn from older saints as they faithfully walk through such pain.

Death and Genesis 1–3

- How does the opening phrase of Genesis, "In the beginning," inform how we understand death?

  The very first words of the Bible are "in the beginning," and the word that immediately follows that phrase is "God." Before anything in our world existed, God existed. There was never a time when He did not exist; nor is there a time when He will cease to exist. There is no death in God, and He even created all things out of nothing; He is a God who gives life.

- How did God make man?

  God made man after His own image, both male and female, and called them to be fruitful and multiply. The living God created a world teeming with life with the potential to produce more life. Furthermore, God created man in two stages. First, God formed the man's body out of the dust of the ground, and then God breathed into him the breath of life, making man body and soul.

- What are two defining features of death as the penalty for sin?

  One of the undeniable empirical truths of this life is that all people die. When Adam sinned, he brought death into the world as sin's penalty, and in Adam, all have sinned. Death is then universal, and more than this, it is cosmic. Adam's sin did not affect humans alone. God also pronounced a curse on the ground, subjecting creation to futility and the bondage of corruption (see Rom. 8:20–21).

After the Video

- What do you consider to be the most problematic trends in culture and the church that take us away from serious reflection about death and why?

  In many ways, we can be saddened that trends emerge in the church that would take Christians away from sober reflection on death and dying, especially with Christ's death and resurrection at the heart of our faith. Whether it is consumerism, entertainment-driven worship, or separation of people within congregations, there are issues that need to be addressed. But there are also larger cultural influences, and answers to this question require some critical thought to identify what problems loom larger.

- Why is it important to affirm that death is the penalty for sin?

  There are many reasons why it is important to affirm that death is the penalty for sin. Not only is this true, but it is integral for a proper understanding of the gospel. In this lecture, Dr. Waters emphasized that the alternative to affirming that death is the penalty for sin is the belief that death is natural, that creatures die because that's just the way things are. Yet death is not natural, and it was not part of God's very good creation.

- Which of the five basic truths about death from Genesis 1–3 stuck out to you the most in driving home the unnaturalness of death or the grievousness of sin?

  The five basic truths about death from Genesis 1–3 related to who God is and the liveliness of His creation, God's creation of man as body and soul, death as sin's penalty, the universal nature of death, and the cosmic nature of death. The answers to this question, which will vary, should weigh these five basic truths in terms of the unnaturalness of death and the grievousness of sin.

REVIEW QUIZ

1. **C.**

   Though Dr. Waters did mention our culture's love for and glorification of violence, it is ironic how our culture suppresses the reality of death. On the one hand, our culture distances us from experience with death because our loved ones no longer die at home, as was once customary; entertainment keeps us distracted from ultimate realities; and people cope with death in new ways, as seen in trends at funeral and memorial ceremonies. On the other hand, our culture glories in violence, which should bring the reality of death more to mind, though perhaps it trivializes it.

2. **B.**

   Dr. Waters noted a recent survey that documented the most popular songs at funerals. These songs were well-known secular songs. No classic hymns made the top ten of this survey's list.

3. **D.**

   It is not surprising to find that some of the things that distract and distance people from death in our culture are paralleled by trends in the church. Just as there seem to be endless forms of entertainment to distract us in the culture, the church has embraced entertainment, which changes the character of our worship. Likewise, the distancing of loved ones at the end of their lives is paralleled by the separation of people in churches by their ages and stages of life.

4. **C.**

   Adam knew that death was the penalty for sin before he ate from the Tree of Knowledge of Good and Evil. God had warned Adam, "You may surely eat of every tree of the garden, but of the tree of the knowledge of good and evil you shall not eat, for in the day that you eat of it you shall surely die" (Gen. 2:16–17).

5. **A.**

   When one understands that death is the penalty for sin, it cannot be explained away as natural or just the way things are. Genesis 1 especially wars against this view of death and dying. The living God created a living creation that itself could produce life. There is no hint of death in Genesis 1, and God saw that His creation was not just "good" but "very good."

6. **D.**
These passages can be connected to the basic truths of Genesis 1–3 concerning death because death is universal in scope and the wages of sin, and we all have sinned in Adam. The passage from Romans 8 in particular was quoted to connect the cosmic nature of death; death as the wages of sin has affected not only humankind but all creation.

2

What Is Death? Three Complementary Truths

INTRODUCTION

Genesis 1–3 immediately focuses our attention on matters of life and death. This fact teaches us that God takes these matters seriously and that we ought to take them seriously as well. In this lesson, Dr. Waters expands on the five principles of death from Genesis 1–3, adding three complementary truths that help us to further define death as a multidimensional, a certain, and—apart from Christ—a fearful reality.

LEARNING GOALS

When you have finished this lesson, you should be able to:

- Provide a definition for death
- Describe the three scriptural dimensions of death
- Explain why death is a certainty in this life

KEY IDEAS

- Death must be understood multidimensionally from natural, spiritual, and eternal perspectives.
- Adam was the appointed representative of all his natural descendants, such that from the moment when we begin to exist, we are guilty of Adam's sin and liable to God's judgment.
- Death is a fearful thing, and to be delivered from the bondage of its fear, we need to be reconciled to God through Jesus Christ.

REFLECTION & DISCUSSION QUESTIONS

Before the Video

What Do You Think?

Take a moment to answer the following questions. They will prepare you for the lecture.

- Are you afraid to die? Why or why not?

- Have you ever questioned the fairness of Adam's sin and its implications?

Scripture Reading

Someone in the crowd said to him, "Teacher, tell my brother to divide the inheritance with me." But he said to him, "Man, who made me a judge or arbitrator over you?" And he said to them, "Take care, and be on your guard against all covetousness, for one's life does not consist in the abundance of his possessions." And he told them a parable, saying, "The land of a rich man produced plentifully, and he thought to himself, 'What shall I do, for I have nowhere to store my crops?' And he said, 'I will do this: I will tear down my barns and build larger ones, and there I will store all my grain and my goods. And I will say to my soul, "Soul, you have ample goods laid up for many years; relax, eat, drink, be merry."' But God said to him, 'Fool! This night your soul is required of you, and the things you have prepared, whose will they be?' So is the one who lays up treasure for himself and is not rich toward God."

—Luke 12:13–21

- How does this parable teach us that our days are numbered by God?

During the Video

Answer the following questions while you watch the video. They will guide you through the lecture.

Dimensions of Death *0:00–7:30*

- What is death, naturally speaking?

- What is eternal death, and what is its sad reality?

The Certainty of Death *7:30–17:35*

- Why is death certain?

- How did God relate to Adam? How does Adam relate to us?

The Fear of Death *17:35–24:04*

- What does the fear of death result in for the unbeliever?

- Why is death fearful apart from Christ?

After the Video

Answer the following questions after you have finished the lecture. They will help you identify and summarize the major points.

- How does spiritual death relate to the world, the flesh, and the devil?

  If you are in a group, have the members read Ephesians 2:1–10. Ask: How does God's work for us in Christ change our relationship to the world, the flesh, and the devil?

- Why is God's covenantal relationship with Adam and the results of its being broken not unjust or unfair?

  If you are in a group, have the members imagine that someone has raised the accusation that God has been unjust and that it is unfair for people to be held accountable for Adam's sin. Ask: How could we share the gospel if this accusation were raised?

- Why is death a rich opportunity for sharing the gospel?

  If you are in a group, have the members share their experiences with others who were near the end of life or fearful of death. Ask: How were the circumstances fruitful for sharing the gospel? What made sharing the gospel easier or more difficult during those situations?

PRAYER

Commit what you have learned from God's Word in this lesson to prayer.

- Praise God for His unchanging nature and covenant faithfulness.
- Confess any frustrations that you might have about your guilt of Adam's sin.
- Thank God for sending His Son into the world as a new Adam and the righteous Mediator of the covenant of grace.
- Ask God to help you fix your eyes on Jesus Christ, resting in His righteousness, so as to deliver you from any fear of death that you might experience in this life.

REVIEW QUIZ

Use these multiple-choice questions to measure what you learned from this lesson.

1. Which of the following is *not* one of the three dimensions of death?
   a. Certain
   b. Eternal
   c. Natural
   d. Spiritual

2. The natural dimension of death deals with the naturalness of death as part of God's creation.
   a. True
   b. False

3. What is a good response to the idea that the guilt of Adam's sin was unfair to place on our account?
   a. God had the right to covenant with Adam as Creator.
   b. God was exceedingly generous to Adam in the garden.
   c. We are also guilty of our own sin and not only Adam's.
   d. All of the above

4. What is Paul's ultimate purpose in speaking about Adam in Romans 5 and 1 Corinthians 15?
   a. To answer why we die
   b. To point to the work of Christ
   c. To call us to works of righteousness
   d. To explain the futility of creation

5. The bondage of the fear of death is something that everyone experiences equally.
   a. True
   b. False

6. What analogy was provided to illustrate how death is fearful to unbelievers?
    a. Death as eternal sleep
    b. Death as crossing the Jordan
    c. Death as the popularized Grim Reaper
    d. Death as a warrant for an arrest

Answer Key—What Is Death? Three Complementary Truths

REFLECTION & DISCUSSION QUESTIONS

Before the Video

What Do You Think?

These are personal questions. The answers should be based on your own knowledge and experience.

Scripture Reading

- How does this parable teach us that our days are numbered by God?

  This parable underscores the dangers of covetousness, especially in light of the truth that our days have been numbered. Just as God knows the hairs on our heads, He knows the number of our days, as seen in this parable when God says: "Fool! This night your soul is required of you." The implication of God's appointing our day of death is that He has also appointed the days of our lives.

During the Video

Dimensions of Death

- What is death, naturally speaking?

  Death is not natural. It was not originally a part of God's good creation. But death does strike at our natures as soul and body. Death, therefore, is defined as the separation or rending of the soul from the body.

- What is eternal death, and what is its sad reality?

  Eternal death is described by Jesus as "eternal punishment" (Matt. 25:46) and in Revelation as the "second death" (20:14). Eternal death is what follows natural death and spiritual death apart from Christ. The sad reality in eternity for those who were rebellious against God is that nothing changes about this state of rebellion when God justly judges them for it.

The Certainty of Death

- Why is death certain?

  The certainty of death finds its basis in God's eternal and unchanging decree, that God has appointed that all people will die (Heb. 9:27). God is just, and He has purposed that all should die on account of sin.

- How did God relate to Adam? How does Adam relate to us?

  God entered into a covenant relationship with Adam, and Adam represented all his natural descendants in this covenant relationship, such that when Adam sinned, we sinned. Adam's sin was counted to us, and so we are liable to God's just judgment of that sin, of which death is the penalty.

The Fear of Death

- What does the fear of death result in for the unbeliever?

  For the unbeliever, the fear of death results in a lifelong slavery to it. Jesus came to "deliver all those who through fear of death were subject to lifelong slavery" (Heb. 2:15). Only in Christ can we be delivered from the fear of death.

- Why is death fearful apart from Christ?

  Death is fearful for many reasons. Though our deaths are fixed in the decree of God, we don't know when our deaths will come. Also, death is loss; it takes away everything that is familiar to us in this world. But what makes death most fearful for the unbeliever in particular is that it is the penalty of sin, and through it, the unbeliever is brought into the presence of our holy Judge.

After the Video

- How does spiritual death relate to the world, the flesh, and the devil?

  Spiritual death is the death that holds sway in our lives even before we are deceased. Paul describes us as being "dead in . . . trespasses and sins" apart from Christ (Eph. 2:1). Being spiritually dead, people do not serve God, but serve the world, the flesh, and the devil. We put our bodies in the service of sin, running away from God and running into sin with all the encouragement of the world and of Satan (see Eph. 2:1–3).

- Why is God's covenantal relationship with Adam and the results of its being broken not unjust or unfair?

  Often when people hear that they are themselves guilty of Adam's sin, they raise the objection that this is unfair and even that God is unjust. But God had every right as Creator to enter into covenant with Adam, and man alone of all of God's creatures enjoyed this covenant relationship. Furthermore, God was unspeakably generous with Adam in the garden, having abundantly provided for him. In all this, we still sin against God. Our actions speak louder than words, and our protests ring hollow if we actively love our sin.

- Why is death a rich opportunity for sharing the gospel?

  Death is a particularly rich opportunity for sharing the gospel because it can provide an easy avenue to draw a person's attention to the reality of sin and also to the Savior. The gospel is the remedy not only for the fear of death but for the penalty of sin—death itself. Through Jesus Christ, we are made spiritually alive, and though we still experience natural death, we are delivered from the bondage of the fear of death, knowing that when we die, we will be brought into the presence of Christ and will not experience eternal death.

REVIEW QUIZ

1. **A.**
   The certainty of death was a main point of this lesson, but it was not one of the three dimensions of death, which are natural death, spiritual death, and eternal death.

2. **B.**
   Death is not natural to God's original creation. It was introduced as the penalty for sin. The natural dimension of death concerns the reality that death strikes at our natures as creatures who are body and soul.

3. **D.**
   The idea that we are guilty of Adam's sin and that death entered the world on account of his sin often prompts the objection that God's arrangement with Adam was unfair. But God's right as Creator, His goodness toward Adam, and our own sinfulness are ways that Dr. Waters addressed this charge.

4. **B.**
   One of the most blessed realities to reflect on when thinking about the devastation of Adam's sin and our guilt in Adam is that we are justified only by the works of Another—the works of Jesus Christ. Pointing to this truth is Paul's ultimate purpose when he speaks about Adam in Romans 5 and 1 Corinthians 15.

5. **B.**
   Not everyone experiences this bondage to the fear of death equally. The believer in Jesus Christ is delivered from the bondage to the fear of death, while the unbeliever is still in subjection to it.

6. **D.**
   Dr. Waters used the analogy of death as an arrest warrant to explain why death is ultimately fearful to unbelievers. Death arrests someone into the presence of our most holy Judge to whom that person must give an account for his or her lifelong rebellion against Him.

3

What Happens after Death?

INTRODUCTION

One of the reasons that death can be so fearful is the uncertainty that many face about what happens when we die. Christians can have certainty about this through the Bible, but there are many unbiblical answers to the question "What happens after death?" False viewpoints exist. In this lesson, Dr. Waters answers this question from a biblical perspective and deals with unbiblical beliefs about what happens when we die.

LEARNING GOALS

When you have finished this lesson, you should be able to:

- Explain what happens after we die, according to the Bible
- Address unbiblical answers that we hear in the church and in the world about what happens after death

KEY IDEAS

- We must be reconciled to God in this life before death, or we will enter eternity as God's enemies without any opportunity for salvation.
- The Roman Catholic doctrine of purgatory is unbiblical and is based on an unbiblical view of justification.
- At death, the souls of believers are made perfectly holy, and their bodies are committed to the grave, where they await the resurrection, even still being united to Christ.

REFLECTION & DISCUSSION QUESTIONS

Before the Video

What Do You Think?

Take a moment to answer the following questions. They will prepare you for the lecture.

- What are some popular beliefs about what happens when we die?

- Do you struggle with uncertainty about what happens when we die? How might the truth of the gospel help you or someone else who struggles with this uncertainty?

Scripture Reading

There was a rich man who was clothed in purple and fine linen and who feasted sumptuously every day. And at his gate was laid a poor man named Lazarus, covered with sores, who desired to be fed with what fell from the rich man's table. Moreover, even the dogs came and licked his sores. The poor man died and was carried by the angels to Abraham's side. The rich man also died and was buried, and in Hades, being in torment, he lifted up his eyes and saw Abraham far off and Lazarus at his side. And he called out, "Father Abraham, have mercy on me, and send Lazarus to dip the end of his finger in water and cool my tongue, for I am in anguish in this flame." But Abraham said, "Child, remember that you in your lifetime received your good things, and Lazarus in like manner bad things; but now he is comforted here, and you are in anguish. And besides all this, between us and you a great chasm has been fixed, in order that those who would pass from here to you may not be able, and none may cross from there to us." And he said, "Then I beg you, father, to send him to my father's house—for I have five brothers—so that he may warn them, lest they also come into this place of torment." But Abraham said, "They have Moses and the Prophets; let them hear them." And he said, "No, father Abraham, but if someone goes to them from the dead, they will repent." He said to him, "If they do not hear Moses and the Prophets, neither will they be convinced if someone should rise from the dead."

—Luke 16:19–31

- What does Jesus' teaching inform us about life after death?

During the Video

Answer the following questions while you watch the video. They will guide you through the lecture.

Unbiblical Views *0:00–16:23*

- What is universalism? In what sense is salvation universal?

- What is annihilationism, and why is it unbiblical?

- Do we get a second chance when we die? Why or why not?

- How does the doctrine of purgatory relate to Rome's teaching on justification?

Scriptural Truth *16:23–23:57*

- What happens to believers, soul and body, when they die?

- What happens to people who die in rebellion against God?

After the Video

Answer the following questions after you have finished the lecture. They will help you identify and summarize the major points.

- Why would universalists appeal to the love of God as a foundation of their belief? Is this a sufficient reason to believe universalism? Why or why not?

  If you are in a group, have the members consider how their Christian life might be different if they were universalists. Ask: Would you evangelize people? Would you pursue holiness?

- Of the unbiblical teachings about what happens after death, which do you consider to be most problematic and why? What do these views share in common?

  If you are in a group, have the members discuss their answers to the questions above and the various commonalities between these unbiblical views that they may have found.

- How ought the truth of what happens after we die affect the way we respond to it and live in light of it right now?

  If you are in a group, have the members read 2 Thessalonians 1. Ask: How does Paul call us to live in light of the return of Christ? What about Paul's teaching astounds you most?

PRAYER

Commit what you have learned from God's Word in this lesson to prayer.

- Praise God for His loving nature and desire to save though He would have been perfectly just to condemn us in our sin.
- Confess any lack of watchfulness or bad stewardship even though you know the truth that Jesus will return suddenly.
- Thank God for the Bible and the certain truth contained within it about what will happen to us when we die.
- Ask God to give you a great zeal for holiness and for the salvation of the lost.

REVIEW QUIZ

Use these multiple-choice questions to measure what you learned from this lesson.

1. What is the intermediate state?
   a. The period before certainty about what happens after death
   b. The period that is spent in purgatory before going to heaven
   c. The period between a person's death and the return of Christ
   d. The period of testing or probation for a second chance for salvation

2. Scripture does teach that salvation is universal in a limited sense, but it rejects universalism, the teaching that all people will be saved.
   a. True
   b. False

3. Which of the following unbiblical views of what happens after death must be denied because of the return of Christ in judgment?
   a. Annihilationism and second probation
   b. Second probation and purgatory
   c. Universalism and annihilationism
   d. Universalism and second probation

4. Which of the following unbiblical views of what happens after death was connected to the doctrine of justification?
   a. Annihilationism
   b. Purgatory
   c. Second probation
   d. Universalism

5. After the souls of believers enter heaven, our bodies are no longer significant.
   a. True
   b. False

6. What is our great hope after death?
   a. To be free from the body
   b. To enter Christ's presence
   c. To leave the pain of this world
   d. To reunite with our loved ones

Answer Key—What Happens after Death?

REFLECTION & DISCUSSION QUESTIONS

Before the Video

What Do You Think?

These are personal questions. The answers should be based on your own knowledge and experience.

Scripture Reading

- What does Jesus' teaching inform us about life after death?

  The parables of Jesus are drawn from reality. This parable teaches us that there is indeed life after death. It also teaches us that we will be consciously aware of our eternal state. In the case of the rich man, he describes his condition in a "place of torment" and has an awareness that he cannot escape this place. Jesus connects this man's eternal state in Hades with how he lived unjustly in this life.

During the Video

Unbiblical Views

- What is universalism? In what sense is salvation universal?

  Universalism is the belief that everyone will be saved. Some universalists believe that everyone will be saved by following their own religion, while others believe that everyone will ultimately be saved by the work of Christ. While universalism is not true, the Bible does teach that salvation is universal in the sense that people from all tribes, tongues, and nations will be saved. Salvation is universal in that it is not the exclusive privilege of any one group.

- What is annihilationism, and why is it unbiblical?

  Annihilationism is the belief that God will indeed execute judgment on the wicked, but the wicked will cease to exist on account of that judgment. Annihilationism allows for only two options: salvation and nonexistence. This view is unbiblical because the Bible teaches that people experience a conscious existence after death. The parable of the rich man and Lazarus is a classic text that challenges annihilationism.

- Do we get a second chance when we die? Why or why not?

  We do not get a second chance to repent and believe in Jesus Christ when we die. The Bible teaches that a person's eternal destiny is measured by life on earth and not by something that happens after death. We are judged by what we have done in this one bodily life: "For we must all appear before the judgment seat of

Christ, so that each one may receive what is due for what he has done in the body, whether good or evil" (2 Cor. 5:10).

- How does the doctrine of purgatory relate to Rome's teaching on justification?

  Purgatory is the place where Christians go after death, according to the Roman Catholic Church, to be purged of any remaining unrighteousness before going to heaven. Belief in purgatory is logically connected to Rome's beliefs about justification, in which a person is declared righteous not by faith alone in Christ alone but by the person's being made actually righteous, and thus justifiable, in this life. Because this process is seldom completed in this life, purgatory is needed so that a person can be truly righteous and enter heaven.

Scriptural Truth

- What happens to believers, soul and body, when they die?

  God saves us body and soul. When we die, our souls are made perfectly holy in heaven (Heb. 12:23), where we are present with Christ (2 Cor. 5:6–8; Phil. 1:23). Though our souls are in heaven, our bodies remain in the grave, yet they are still united to Christ and await redemption (Rom. 8:23, 1 Thess. 4:16). When we are raised from the dead, we will dwell with the Lord as redeemed whole persons.

- What happens to people who die in rebellion against God?

  Unlike the souls of believers, who go to be with the Lord in heaven, the souls of those who are still enemies of God are cast into hell, into a place of utter darkness and conscious torment. What Jude says of the fallen angels who are "kept in eternal chains under gloomy darkness until the judgment of the great day" (v. 6) is also true of wicked human beings.

After the Video

- Why would universalists appeal to the love of God as a foundation of their belief? Is this a sufficient reason to believe universalism? Why or why not?

  The love of God should surprise us, and we ought not to pit God's love and His righteousness against each other. Throughout Scripture, God's love is looked to as the reason that the Son of God came into the world (John 3:16; 1 John 4:9). For a universalist, universal salvation is consistent with such a great love, yet this overlooks plain scriptural teaching and the righteous character of God. The Bible teaches that all have sinned (Rom. 3:23), and this state of rebellion does not end at death. This rebellion is brought to an end in this life only through the one way of salvation: faith in Christ alone. This salvation is possible only before Christ returns in judgment to separate the sheep from the goats (Matt. 25:31–46), ushering some into eternal life and others into eternal death.

- Of the unbiblical teachings about what happens after death, which do you consider to be most problematic and why? What do these views share in common?

The answer to this question considers the unbiblical views in this lecture about what happens after death (universalism, annihilationism, second probation, and purgatory) in terms of which is most problematic. This may be difficult to determine in that each of these views is unbiblical—a core commonality. Other commonalities might include a shallow view of the work of Christ and a failure to understand God's character.

- How ought the truth of what happens after we die affect the way we respond to it and live in light of it right now?

  The answers to this question may vary, but at the end of this lecture, Dr. Waters made some application of these truths to our lives. Scripture impresses on us the finality of death but also the good news that there is salvation in Jesus Christ. Our calling as Christians is to make Christ known. We might not be called to preach, but we can pray and support the church while sharing the gospel with others whenever the Lord provides us with opportunity. We must be reminded that the whole of our lives is a pilgrimage, and we must be faithful along the way.

REVIEW QUIZ

1. **C.**
   Broadly, the intermediate state is the period between a person's death and the return of Christ. It is the period in which the soul exists apart from the body. There are many unbiblical explanations of what happens during this state, such as purgatory, but the intermediate state is a broader category and applies to all people.

2. **A.**
   Salvation is universal in scope, and the Bible emphasizes this point. All types of people from every nation will be saved without exclusion. This does not mean that all people will be saved without exception.

3. **D.**
   When Christ returns, the dead will be raised, and He will execute judgment on all people. Christ's return marks the end of the intermediate state. Since purgatory is an attempted explanation of what happens during the intermediate state, the fact of Christ's return does not disprove the belief in purgatory. Likewise, Christ's return in judgment does not disprove annihilationism, because it is believed that annihilation would be a result of Christ's judgment. Christ's return in judgment does, however, disprove universalism (since some will be condemned) and the belief in a second probation (since Christ makes judgment against the deeds done in the body, which means that the opportunity of salvation ends at a person's death).

4. **B.**
   Though a valid connection to the doctrine of justification may be made to any of these views, Dr. Waters connected the Roman Catholic belief in purgatory to Rome's understanding of justification. Rome teaches that a person is made justifiable in

this life but that this process is seldom perfect, so purgatory is necessary to make someone perfectly righteous and admissible into heaven.

5. **B.**
Though our souls are separated from our bodies during the intermediate state, our bodies are still united to Christ. Using 1 Thessalonians 4:14 as support, Westminster Shorter Catechism 37 states: "The souls of believers are at their death made perfect in holiness, and do immediately pass into glory; and their bodies, being still united to Christ, do rest in their graves, till the resurrection."

6. **B.**
Freedom from the body is not a Christian hope unless it is connected to the pains of the body and our tendencies to use the body for sin. God made us body and soul. But when our souls are separated from our bodies at death, our great hope is to enter the presence of Christ. This was Paul's great hope: "My desire is to depart and be with Christ" (Phil. 1:23).

4

Why Did Christ Die?

INTRODUCTION

The life, death, and resurrection of Jesus Christ mean everything. To understand why Christ came and why He died is to understand the gospel, and to understand and trust in Jesus Christ as He is offered in the gospel is to have rich assurance in the face of death. In this lesson, Dr. Waters answers the question "Why did Christ die?" and explains why it is vital to be united to Him in His life, death, and resurrection.

LEARNING GOALS

When you have finished this lesson, you should be able to:

- Answer the question "Why did Christ die?"
- Define what it means to be united to Christ
- Explain why being united to Christ redefines the meaning of death for believers

KEY IDEAS

- Every believer is united to Christ, who united Himself to our humanity and indwells us by His Spirit through faith.
- Christ's life of obedience, death as a sacrifice for sin, and resurrection for our justification give us full victory over death.

REFLECTION & DISCUSSION QUESTIONS

Before the Video

What Do You Think?

Take a moment to answer the following questions. They will prepare you for the lecture.

- What type of life did Jesus live? Why is it strange that He should die?

- Why did Christ die?

Scripture Reading

Since therefore the children share in flesh and blood, he himself likewise partook of the same things, that through death he might destroy the one who has the power of death, that is, the devil, and deliver all those who through fear of death were subject to lifelong slavery.

—Hebrews 2:14–15

- According to this passage, why did the Son of God become a man?

During the Video

Answer the following questions while you watch the video. They will guide you through the lecture.

Union with Christ *0:00–10:25*

- What did Christ first do that makes our union with Him possible?

- What are two things that we ought to think about in relation to our union with Christ?

Christ's Life, Death, and Resurrection *10:25–23:30*

- What is the one thing that marked the life of Christ? To what extent did it mark His life?

- What did Christ accomplish in His death on the cross?

- Why was Christ raised, and what happened to death at the resurrection?

After the Video

Answer the following questions after you have finished the lecture. They will help you identify and summarize the major points.

- Using the themes of this lesson in relation to death, answer: What is the gospel?

  If you are in a group, have the members read Romans 5:1–11. Ask: Why are these truths a firm foundation for hope when we die?

- What do Christ's life, death, and resurrection individually mean for us who are united to Him?

  If you are in a group, have the members discuss why each aspect of Christ's life, death, and resurrection matters. Ask: What would it be like if we had only one or two without the other(s)?

- Are you "in Christ"? How can you know? Why is this question critical to ask in the face of death?

  If you are in a group, have the members read John 15. Ask: How does this passage relate to union with Christ? How should our lives look in union with Christ?

PRAYER

Commit what you have learned from God's Word in this lesson to prayer.

- Praise God for His love in sending His Son into the world.
- Confess areas in your life that are not presently characterized by the Spirit.
- Thank God that He did not spare His only Son, though He was perfectly obedient, so that He would be raised from the dead for our justification.
- Ask God to impress on you the reality that hope in the face of death is only in Christ so that you might tell others more zealously about the beauty of being united to Him.

REVIEW QUIZ

Use these multiple-choice questions to measure what you learned from this lesson.

1. Which of the following is the valid contradiction of terms from this lecture?
   a. Three in one
   b. Faith and works
   c. God-man Jesus Christ
   d. Crossless Christianity

2. Which of the following offices of Christ was emphasized?
   a. Judge
   b. Prophet
   c. High Priest
   d. King

3. Jesus could have accomplished our salvation from heaven.
   a. True
   b. False

4. What is the primary reason that Christ died on the cross?
   a. To provide an example
   b. To picture the sinfulness of sin
   c. To demonstrate the love of God
   d. To be a sacrifice for our sin

5. Christ's resurrection has little to do with our justification, unlike His death.
   a. True
   b. False

6. Which is *not* one of the major points of what Christ's life, death, and resurrection mean for us who are united to Him?
   a. Death is powerless for the believer on account of His work.
   b. Our sinlessness is the measure of our gratitude for His work.
   c. The resurrection verdict of righteousness is ours because of His work.
   d. We have the sure hope of life because of His obedience to His Father.

Answer Key—Why Did Christ Die?

REFLECTION & DISCUSSION QUESTIONS

Before the Video

What Do You Think?

These are personal questions. The answers should be based on your own knowledge and experience.

Scripture Reading

- According to this passage, why did the Son of God become a man?

  A sobering truth is that God hands us over to our sins when we suppress the truth about Him and become idolaters. In Romans 1:18, Paul says that this is a revelation of God's wrath, that even our sin is an expression of His judgment.

During the Video

Union with Christ

- What did Christ first do that makes our union with Him possible?

  Every believer can be united to Christ because He first united Himself to our humanity. The second person of the Godhead united His deity to a true human nature. In the incarnation, God became a man without ceasing to be God.

- What are two things that we ought to think about in relation to our union with Christ?

  We should think about our union with Christ in terms of the ministry of the Holy Spirit and our faith. It is through the Holy Spirit that Christ indwells us, and the Spirit unites us to Christ through faith, such that faith is the bond of our union to Christ.

Christ's Life, Death, and Resurrection

- What is the one thing that marked the life of Christ? To what extent did it mark His life?

  The one thing that marked the life of Jesus Christ was obedience. His primary mission was to do the will of the Father (see John 4:34; 17:4), and He was obedient to the Father all His life, even to the point of His death on the cross (see Phil. 2:8).

- What did Christ accomplish in His death on the cross?

  Christ did not die simply to set an example of what it means to self-sacrificially love another. He died to be our sacrifice for sin, and it is by His blood, the purchase price of our redemption, that we have been delivered. Through His death, the wrath of God has been propitiated, for Christ became sin so that we might be made righteous (2 Cor. 5:21).

- Why was Christ raised, and what happened to death at the resurrection?

  Paul teaches us what the purpose of Christ's resurrection is for us: Jesus was "raised for our justification" (Rom. 4:25). At the resurrection, the sentence of death itself was canceled, and the Father publicly vindicated Jesus Christ and demonstrated that He was the Son of God in power through the resurrection (Rom. 1:4).

After the Video

- Using the themes of this lesson in relation to death, answer: What is the gospel?

  The answer to this question is critical, and the question "What is the gospel?" can be answered with different emphases, such as on the kingdom of God or, in the case of this lecture, as it relates to death. Answers to this question should take into consideration what death is as the penalty for sin and connect it to the life, death, and resurrection of Jesus Christ as that which gives us victory over death and over the condemnation of eternal judgment for our sins.

- What do Christ's life, death, and resurrection individually mean for us who are united to Him?

  In our union with Christ, His life, death, and resurrection mean everything to us who believe. By His perfectly obedient life, we, too, have life. Adam forfeited life, but Jesus as the second Adam won life, and through His life, we can have sure hope of everlasting life. By His sacrificial death, we can know that death and the devil have been publicly put to shame as powerless over those who believe. Because Jesus paid the penalty for our sin, death no longer has any claim over us. Finally, by His resurrection, we have certainty that the sentence of death had been nullified such that we will one day be raised from the dead, sharing in the same resurrection verdict of righteousness as Jesus Christ in our union with Him.

- Are you "in Christ"? How can you know? Why is this question critical to ask in the face of death?

  Dr. Waters concluded this lesson with one of the most important applications that we can take away from studying the great benefits of being united in Christ in the face of death. You must ask yourself, "Am I in Christ?" It is only through union with Christ that we can be delivered, so we must examine ourselves if we are trusting in Jesus Christ alone and ask ourselves whether the work of the Spirit is present in our lives and giving us the mindset of the Spirit to walk in His ways. Our works in step with the Spirit do not earn our salvation and deliver us from death, but they point us to the reality of our union to the One who did.

REVIEW QUIZ

1. **D.**
   Christianity finds its center and focus on the death of Jesus Christ. There would be no Christianity and thus no salvation without the cross of Jesus Christ, which is why crossless Christianity *is a contradiction in terms.*

2. **C.**
   Christ's office as Priest, and most specifically as High Priest, was emphasized in this lesson in connection with Hebrews 2. The High Priestly Prayer of John 17 was also mentioned. Jesus became as one of us so that He might be our Great High Priest and offer Himself as the propitiation for our sins.

3. **B.**
   Jesus could not have been our High Priest if He had not become like one of us. Hebrews 2 tells us: "Therefore he had to be made like his brothers in every respect, so that he might become a merciful and faithful high priest in the service of God, to make propitiation for the sins of the people" (v. 17).

4. **D.**
   While certainly the Son came into the world and died on the cross as a demonstration of God's love (John 3:16; Rom. 5:8; 1 John 4:10), He did not die merely to be an example of self-sacrificial love. Furthermore, God's love in not sparing His own Son was for a purpose: that He might be the sacrifice for our sin.

5. **B.**
   Romans 4:24–25 tells us: "[Righteousness] will be counted to us who believe in him who raised from the dead Jesus our Lord, who was delivered up for our trespasses and raised for our justification." Christ's resurrection, and not merely His death, is intimately connected to our justification.

6. **B.**
   In the Christian life, the power of sin is broken by the Holy Spirit, but we still experience sin's presence. Though striving after holiness is an expression of gratitude for Christ's work, perfection is not the mark of our gratitude. Yet we strive for holiness in the reality that Christ's obedient life gives us sure hope of life, that His death has abolished death and the one who held the power of it, and that His resurrection frees us from all condemnation.

5

Why Do Christians Die?

INTRODUCTION

If death is the penalty for sin, and Jesus died to pay that penalty for us as Christians, then why do we still die? This is a valid question, and considering that death is a fearful thing, it is also an important one. What must we keep in mind in asking this question? In this lesson, Dr. Waters helps us see that although Christians experience death, there is comfort in Christ's transformation of death for believers such that death, as strange as it may sound, is an expression of God's love for us because of what it brings us into.

LEARNING GOALS

When you have finished this lesson, you should be able to:

- Identify two biblical convictions that we must maintain when asking, "Why do Christians die?"
- Describe how Jesus Christ has transformed death for the Christian: what He has taken from it and added to it
- Name some of our fears about death and their gospel remedies

KEY IDEAS

- Scripture does not answer every one of our questions, but it gives us enough so that we can trust our God fully and confidently as we walk with and before Him even into death.
- The sting and the curse of death have been removed for every believer, and death can be understood as something that God has appointed for our good.
- Death remains an enemy, and the world, the flesh, and the devil will exploit the reality of death to draw us away from God.

REFLECTION & DISCUSSION QUESTIONS

Before the Video

What Do You Think?

Take a moment to answer the following questions. They will prepare you for the lecture.

- Why do Christians still die?
- What do you fear most about death?

Scripture Reading

The righteous man perishes, and no one lays it to heart; devout men are taken away, while no one understands. For the righteous man is taken away from calamity; he enters into peace; they rest in their beds who walk in their uprightness.

—Isaiah 57:1–2

- How does this passage help you consider the nature of death for the righteous?

During the Video

Answer the following questions while you watch the video. They will guide you through the lecture.

The Transformation of Death *0:00–13:42*

- What two biblical convictions must we hold that lead to the question "Why do Christians die?"
- What has Jesus taken away from death?
- What has Jesus added to death?

Facing Our Fears with the Gospel *13:42–24:04*

- What three fears are commonly faced because of death?

- What truths must we remember in facing those fears?

After the Video

Answer the following questions after you have finished the lecture. They will help you identify and summarize the major points.

- Are you challenged by the idea that the death of believers is out of God's love for us? In what sense does God's love for us shine through even in our deaths?

  If you are in a group, have the members discuss they have ever asked or struggled with the question "Why do Christians die?" Ask: How has this lecture helped you understand the nature of death for the believer more fully?

- Why ought we to think of death more and not less? How ought we to think about the day we die?

  If you are in a group, have the members read Luke 21:34–36 and talk about why reflecting on death can be helpful not only for how we die but also for how we live.

- What are your greatest fears about death? Does the truth of the gospel help ease these fears? Why or why not?

  If you are in a group, have the members discuss what is most fearful about death to them and why. Ask: What practical steps can be taken to help alleviate those fears?

PRAYER

Commit what you have learned from God's Word in this lesson to prayer.

- Praise God as the one living and true God who has given you life.
- Confess ways that you do not live in light of the brevity of life and the call to steward your days for God's glory.
- Thank God that He has appointed even your last day and experience of death for your good.
- Ask God to impress upon you the truths of the gospel so that you are not tempted to despair when facing the fears that so often accompany death.

REVIEW QUIZ

Use these multiple-choice questions to measure what you learned from this lesson.

1. Who wrote *The Death of Death in the Death of Christ*?
   a. Thomas Brooks
   b. Thomas Boston
   c. Martin Luther
   d. John Owen

2. What document was quoted for its answer to the question "Why do Christians die?"
   a. Westminster Confession of Faith
   b. Westminster Larger Catechism
   c. Westminster Shorter Catechism
   d. Westminster Directory of Public Worship

3. As Christians, we still encounter death as an experience and as a state or condition.
   a. True
   b. False

4. Believers are delivered from the sting of death because we encounter death not as the judicial penalty of sin.
   a. True
   b. False

5. What is *not* one of the common fears of death mentioned in this lecture?
   a. Fear of readiness
   b. Fear of pain
   c. Fear of loss
   d. Fear of legacy

6. What is *not* one of the ways prescribed for how we ought to confront death?
   a. To think about death more rather than less
   b. To think about death rationally, apart from emotion
   c. To think about death as bringing us into Christ's presence
   d. To think about death as the laying down of sin and misery

Answer Key—Why Do Christians Die?

REFLECTION & DISCUSSION QUESTIONS

Before the Video

What Do You Think?

These are personal questions. The answers should be based on your own knowledge and experience.

Scripture Reading

- How does this passage help you consider the nature of death for the righteous?

  All the sins of believers are forgiven in Christ. They are righteous in Him, yet they still experience death. In this passage, Isaiah sees death as something welcome for the righteous. He says that the righteous through death "enter into peace," and this is partly because they are delivered from an unrighteous world

During the Video

The Transformation of Death

- What two biblical convictions must we hold that lead to the question "Why do Christians die?"

  The two biblical convictions that we must hold when asking this question concern what death is and what Christ has done. On the one hand, death is the wages of sin; it is something deserved. But on the other hand, we must hold that all the sins of believers are forgiven in Christ. We must hold these two convictions with equal firmness, but they do seem to create a tension about how to understand death and the Christian.

- What has Jesus taken away from death?

  Even though believers experience death, it has been transformed by Christ. He has taken something away from death that changes its nature for Christians. When Christians die, it is not because death is a master over us; we are not undergoing it as a penalty for our sins. Death's sting has been taken from us because we are declared righteous in Christ.

- What has Jesus added to death?

  In transforming death for Christians, not only has Jesus taken something away from death, but He has also added something to it. Death serves a blessed purpose for the Christian such that it is even for our good. Through death, we are brought into a state of perfect righteousness, having been freed from sin. Even better than that, we are brought into the presence of Christ and enjoy greater communion with Him.

Facing Our Fears with the Gospel

- What three fears are commonly faced because of death?

  The three fears that are commonly faced because of death are fear of readiness, loss, and pain. We fear whether we are ready to meet God. We fear the loss of our loved ones and the idea that all the things to which we have devoted our lives, such as our work, will come to an end. We also fear the prospect that our deaths will be particularly painful, wondering whether we can bear such pain when it arrives.

- What truths must we remember in facing those fears?

  For the fear of readiness, we must remember the gospel of grace, that we are accepted and counted righteous such that we are indeed ready to stand before God. For the fear of loss, we must remember that the day of death is something that our loving heavenly Father has appointed so that we can commit even that day in trust to Him. For the fear of pain, we must remember that we are not promised to be delivered from pain in the Christian life but that even Jesus experienced it and will be with us through it.

After the Video

- Are you challenged by the idea that the death of believers is out of God's love for us? In what sense does God's love for us shine through even in our deaths?

  The answer to the first question is personal but should consider how you think about the prospect of death. When you think about dying, are you confident that God loves you even through it? Remember that death for the believer is not payment for sins. Our sins have already been paid for by Christ, and because of His work, we may enter God's presence free from the guilt of our sins and also free from our once-fallen natures, no longing wanting or being able to sin. Since death brings believers into this reality, it can be understood as an expression of God's love for us.

- Why ought we to think of death more and not less? How ought we to think about the day we die?

  The world drives us to distraction, from truly contemplating the reality of death. But Christians ought to think about death more and not less. Thinking about death helps us to ready ourselves for it, and it gives us a good opportunity for deeper reflection on and appreciation for the gospel. Martin Luther said, "You must look to death while you are alive and see sin in the light of grace and hell in the light of heaven, permitting nothing to divert you from that view." Knowing that death brings us out of our sin and into the glory of Christ, we can esteem the day of our death even as our best day (see Eccl. 7:1). Thomas Brooks said, "The believer's last day is his best day."

- What are your greatest fears about death? Does the truth of the gospel help ease these fears? Why or why not?

Three fears that we face about death were named in this lecture: the fear of readiness, loss, and pain. Perhaps one of these fears grips you most, but perhaps you've identified in your answer another fear that you must grapple with. Consider the gospel, especially your righteousness in Christ, as you seek to ready yourself for death.

REVIEW QUIZ

1. **D.**
   Some of these authors were quoted in this lecture, but John Owen was named along with the title of one of his most famous works, The Death of Death in the Death of Christ. *This title helps frame why it is valid for Christians to ask, "In light of what Jesus' death accomplished, why do Christians still die?"*

2. **B.**
   Westminster Larger Catechism 85 states: "Death, being the wages of sin, why are not the righteous delivered from death, seeing all their sins are forgiven in Christ? The righteous shall be delivered from death itself at the last day, and even in death are delivered from the sting and curse of it; so that, although they die, yet it is out of God's love, to free them perfectly from sin and misery, and to make them capable of further communion with Christ in glory, which they then enter upon."

3. **B.**
   Christians experience the physical process of dying, but we are delivered from death as a state or a condition. Death does not have an ultimate power over us because of what Christ has accomplished on our behalf.

4. **A.**
   Jesus has paid the wages of sin that we have earned both in Adam and in our actual transgressions. When we die, we are not paying the penalty for sin but rather are being delivered from death itself and are brought into the fullness of life with Christ in glory.

5. **D.**
   Fearing death in terms of legacy (e.g., how we will be remembered by others, the financial stability of our loved ones, the beneficent dealings of our estate) is legitimate, though it was not mentioned in this lecture. This fear does, however, relate to the fears of readiness and loss.

6. **B.**
   As Christians, we are not called to go through life stoically, devoid of emotions, and we are not called to face death in this manner. Rather, our emotions must be shaped by gospel truth as it relates to death, that we are being brought out of a world marked by sin and misery and into Christ's presence. That's why Dr. Waters called us to equip ourselves for death by thinking about it more and not less.

6

How Do I Face the Death of Others?

INTRODUCTION

The previous lessons defined death biblically, and the next four will help us understand how to face the hard realities of death. When it comes to the death of believers, we are not without hope, yet we must strengthen ourselves with gospel encouragement. But what do we do when an unbelieving loved one dies? In this lesson, Dr. Waters gives us five encouragements with concrete examples and commands in Scripture to show how grieving is natural.

LEARNING GOALS

When you have finished this lesson, you should be able to:

- Apply your knowledge of what death is to your experience of the death of others, both believers and unbelievers
- Provide examples and commands of grieving from Scripture and differentiate between godly and ungodly grief
- Identify the five encouragements that the Apostle Paul gave to the Thessalonians who were struggling with the death of others

KEY IDEAS

- Scripture provides powerful examples and clear commands that teach us how we are to respond to death.
- There is a dividing line between godly grief and ungodly grief.
- Everyone needs to be ready to encourage fellow believers and oneself in the face of death with the gospel.
- The death of unbelievers is a hard providence that we must take to the Lord.

REFLECTION & DISCUSSION QUESTIONS

Before the Video

What Do You Think?

Take a moment to answer the following questions. They will prepare you for the lecture.

- Is it wrong to grieve? Why or why not?

- Have you ever felt hopeless in the face of death? What were the circumstances?

Scripture Reading

> *When I saw him, I fell at his feet as though dead. But he laid his right hand on me, saying, "Fear not, I am the first and the last, and the living one. I died, and behold I am alive forevermore, and I have the keys of Death and Hades."*
>
> —Revelation 1:17–18

- How might this passage instill a confidence and hope in us when our believing loved ones are about to die?

During the Video

Answer the following questions while you watch the video. They will guide you through the lecture.

The Witness of Scripture — *0:00–5:56*

- What is one of Paul's earliest pastoral crises? In what letter does he address it?

- What does Scripture teach us is an appropriate response to death? How does it teach us this?

Godly Grief — *5:56–11:58*

- What is the difference between godly grief and ungodly grief?

- What or who is our foundation for godly grief? Why?

Encouragement and Hardship *11:58–23:40*

- What does Paul call dead believers? How does this encourage godly grief?

- How are we to respond to the deaths of unbelievers?

After the Video

Answer the following questions after you have finished the lecture. They will help you identify and summarize the major points.

- What all can be said about the short gospel phrase of 1 Thessalonians 4:14 that "Jesus died and rose again"?

  If you are in a group, have the members spend time memorizing 1 Thessalonians 4:14.

- Which of the five encouragements from 1 Thessalonians 4 would most sway you to hope in the face of a believing loved one's death? Why?

  If you are in a group, have the members consider the reunions that take place at Christ's return. Ask: Which of your loved ones do you look forward to being reunited with the most? What will make that reunion so sweet?

- In what ways are you striving to do what was called the "best thing" that we can do for someone in the face of our own deaths?

  If you are in a group, have the members discuss how difficult it is to process the death of an unbelieving loved one. Ask: Have you experienced this tangible difference compared with the death of a believer? How did you process it?

PRAYER

Commit what you have learned from God's Word in this lesson to prayer.

- Praise God for the living hope that we have in Christ even in death.
- Confess any bitterness that you might have toward God for the deaths of your loved ones.
- Thank God that He can use difficult circumstances to impress upon people a need for the gospel.
- Ask God to use you as an instrumental part of the conversion of your lost loved ones.

REVIEW QUIZ

Use these multiple-choice questions to measure what you learned from this lesson.

1. Who died in the preeminent example of the appropriateness of grief in the Bible?
   a. Absalom
   b. Joseph
   c. Lazarus
   d. Tabitha

2. The command in Romans 12 to weep with those who weep is directed to Christians and confined to their relationship with other Christians.
   a. True
   b. False

3. What was referenced as evidence of the hopelessness in the face of death during Paul's day?
   a. The diversion of the marketplace
   b. The tombstones of the first century
   c. The sexual licentiousness of the Greeks
   d. The Thessalonian believers

4. What is *not* one of the encouragements to godly grief in 1 Thessalonians 4?
   a. What Christ did for us
   b. Who believers are in death
   c. Reunion with all whom we loved
   d. The first rising of the dead in Christ

5. We ought to pray for our unbelieving loved ones who have died.
   a. True
   b. False

6. Where do we get a pattern for how we ought to respond to the death of unbelieving loved ones?
   a. Christ's teaching on casting pearls
   b. Disciples' shaking dust off their feet
   c. Paul's lesson to the Thessalonians on godly grief
   d. Prayers in the Psalms that wrestle with hard providences

Answer Key—How Do I Face the Death of Others?

REFLECTION & DISCUSSION QUESTIONS

Before the Video

What Do You Think?

These are personal questions. The answers should be based on your own knowledge and experience.

Scripture Reading

- How might this passage instill a confidence and hope in us when our believing loved ones are about to die?

  In this passage, John is beholding Jesus in great fear because of His majesty, but Jesus tells him not to fear because of who He is. The same reasons that John is given for not fearing ought to instruct us in how we cope with the death of believing loved ones. Jesus is "the living one," and He conquered death such that He is "alive forevermore." He is the One who has "the keys of Death and Hades." All who die in Him need not fear death, and we should not fear death for them.

During the Video

The Witness of Scripture

- What is one of Paul's earliest pastoral crises? In what letter does he address it?

  First Thessalonians may be Paul's earliest letter. This tells us that the first pastoral crisis that Paul dealt with was not about a doctrinal dispute, as is the case in another early letter, Galatians, that deals with justification by faith alone and the Mosaic law. In 1 Thessalonians, one of the things that Paul deals with is the consternation of believers who did not know what to think about Christians who were dying.

- What does Scripture teach us is an appropriate response to death? How does it teach us this?

  The simple message of Scripture is that we are to respond to death with grief. We are to grieve death—the deaths of believers and unbelievers alike. Grief is a natural and appropriate response to death, and Scripture teaches us this through examples, such as Jesus' weeping over Lazarus, and commands, such as the call to "weep with those who weep" (Rom. 12:15).

Godly Grief

- What is the difference between godly grief and ungodly grief?

  The major difference between godly grief and ungodly grief is hope. Godly grief is rooted in hopefulness, whereas ungodly grief is devoid of hope altogether. Paul calls us "not [to] grieve as others do who have no hope" (1 Thess. 4:13).

- What or who is our foundation for godly grief? Why?

  Rather than a "what," the foundation for our godly grief is a "who." Jesus Christ is the foundation of our hope in the face of death because of what Jesus Christ has done, that He died and has been raised again. Peter says that we are "born again to a living hope through the resurrection of Jesus Christ from the dead" (1 Peter 1:3). Our hope is ultimately Christ.

Encouragement and Hardship

- What does Paul call dead believers? How does this encourage godly grief?

  In 1 Thessalonians 4, Paul provides two phrases to describe believers who have died: they are "those who have fallen asleep" (vv. 14, 15) and the "dead in Christ" (v. 16). This is encouraging because it reminds us that death does not destroy us and that, even in death, we are united to Christ.

- How are we to respond to the deaths of unbelievers?

  We are to respond to the deaths of unbelievers with grief. When we lose an unbelieving loved one, our grief is compounded because we have no confidence to say that the person died in the Lord, so we must commit our grief to the Lord, bringing this hard providence before Him. While we are not to pray for the dead, we are to draw close to God ourselves and pray that God would use such difficult circumstances to draw those who knew this loved one to faith in Him, knowing that their hope and our hope is the gospel.

After the Video

- What all can be said about the short gospel phrase of 1 Thessalonians 4:14 that "Jesus died and rose again"?

  In 1 Thessalonians 4:14, Paul provides a short summary of the gospel: "We believe that Jesus died and rose again." Taken by itself, it states the facts of Jesus' death and resurrection—but when we know the meaning of His death and resurrection, we can say so much more. In His death, he paid the penalty for sin, taking the curse upon Himself and propitiating the wrath of God such that the devil and his workers have been publicly shamed in Jesus' conquering of death and the grave. In His resurrection, He rose to newness of life for our justification, ascended into heaven, and is right now interceding for us.

- Which of the five encouragements from 1 Thessalonians 4 would most sway you to hope in the face of a believing loved one's death? Why?

This question considers the five encouraging truths of 1 Thessalonians 4 about what we believe and how that helps us to grieve rightly about death. They are, in summary: (1) Christ died and was raised; (2) believers are "in Christ" in death; (3) those dead in Christ will be raised first at His return; (4) Christ reunites us to our bodies and loved ones in His presence; and (5) we will always remain in His presence.

- In what ways are you striving to do what was called the "best thing" that we can do for someone in the face of our own deaths?

  The most important thing that we can do to comfort those whom we know and who are likely to witness our deaths is to assure them of our faith and standing with God by our lives. In doing this, we enable them to grieve with profound hope. This question is designed to prompt your thinking in this direction as you consider your life and how it makes known to others that you are a Christian.

REVIEW QUIZ

1. **C.**
   While David grieved for his sons, Jacob grieved when he thought Joseph had died, and the Apostles grieved over Tabitha—each account teaching us the appropriateness of grief—the preeminent example of grief in Scripture is Jesus' own response to the death of Lazarus. The God-man, Jesus Christ, grieved over the death of a loved one; we ought to feel comfortable in this, too.

2. **B.**
   Though Paul was writing to Christians, we should not limit his statement to the church. His call to weep with those who weep is universal in scope, so we ought to weep in grief and mourning with all people. Such moments of rich sympathy may make way for the gospel.

3. **B.**
   The tombstones of Paul's day give testimony to the fact that death did not elicit a hopeful grief. Examples of these inscriptions: "I was not and I was, I am not and I care not" and "If you want to know who I am, the answer is ash and burnt embers."

4. **C.**
   We must make an important qualification about with whom we will be reunited when Christ returns in glory. If we are alive when Christ returns, He will return with our believing loved ones who died before us. Though we may have loved many who did not love the Lord, we will not spend eternity with them in Christ's presence, which is why grieving the death of unbelieving loved ones is so hard.

5. **B.**
   We ought to commit ourselves in prayer to the Lord during the difficult circumstances of the death of an unbelieving loved one, yet our prayers are not to be for this loved one, as if the person could change his or her standing before God.

6. **D.**
Rather than shrugging off the death of unbelieving loved ones, we are called to grieve, but our grieving process will not be the same as when a believing loved one dies. It will not be marked by the hopefulness of godly grief for that person, though we might take hope in the gospel ourselves. During the hard providences of such a death, we need to consult the Psalms, which provide us with a pattern of what it is to pour our hearts out before God.

7

How Do I Help the Dying & Grieving?

INTRODUCTION

Once we know how to face the death of others, we are better equipped to help others. In 1 Thessalonians 4:18, Paul calls us to "encourage one another with these words"—words of gospel truth. In this lesson, Dr. Waters teaches us how to take up our calling as Christians for those who are dying or near to someone who is dying. Five principles will enable us to better minister to those in need of comfort.

LEARNING GOALS

When you have finished this lesson, you should be able to:

- Apply five principles to minister well to those who are dying
- Apply three principles to minister well to those who are grieving the death of a loved one

KEY IDEAS

- Understand gospel truth helps us to rightly think about death and enables us to speak into the lives of those who are dying with gospel hope and be present with them in a supportive way.
- Believers are not spared troubles and trials, including the trials leading up to death.
- We can encourage the grieving by serving them and even reminding them about their deceased loved ones by sharing delightful stories of their character and, if believers, Christian testimony.

REFLECTION & DISCUSSION QUESTIONS

Before the Video

What Do You Think?

Take a moment to answer the following questions. They will prepare you for the lecture.

- How have you comforted those who were dying or grieving? What has seemed effective?

- Why is there wisdom in sometimes remaining silent in the presence of the dying and grieving?

Scripture Reading

Blessed be the God and Father of our Lord Jesus Christ, the Father of mercies and God of all comfort, who comforts us in all our affliction, so that we may be able to comfort those who are in any affliction, with the comfort with which we ourselves are comforted by God. . . . For we do not want you to be unaware, brothers, of the affliction we experienced in Asia. For we were so utterly burdened beyond our strength that we despaired of life itself. Indeed, we felt that we had received the sentence of death. But that was to make us rely not on ourselves but on God who raises the dead.

—2 Corinthians 1:3–4, 8–9

- How might this passage about the comfort that God gives us in affliction also be applied to ministering to those who are dying or grieving?

During the Video

Answer the following questions while you watch the video. They will guide you through the lecture.

Ministering Well *0:00–14:07*

- What is the best way to prepare ourselves to minister to someone who is dying?

- What is often required in our bearing the burdens of others, even while remaining silent in the face of their suffering?

- What passage in the Bible might cause someone difficulty in accepting a physician's prognosis that death is quickly approaching for someone?

Pointing, Praying, Serving, Speaking *14:07–23:35*

- What is a good way to open up gospel conversations with someone who is about to die? What are some examples of this?

- What three things ought we to do for those who are grieving the death of a loved one?

After the Video

Answer the following questions after you have finished the lecture. They will help you identify and summarize the major points.

- Which of the five principles for ministering to those who are dying do you find to be most helpful at this time and why?

  If you are in a group, have the members imagine that they were at the side of someone who is dying. Ask: What psalm or other passage of Scripture would you read or what hymn would you sing?

- How would you respond to someone who could not accept the coming death of a loved one on account of his or her understanding of James 5:15?

  If you are in a group, have the members share what they remember about ways of answering this understanding of James 5:15 in light of a physician's prognosis of the nearness of death. Ask: Why is it not a matter of faithlessness when we accept and act according to such a prognosis?

- What types of prayers were commended in this lecture for those who are dying? What types of prayers ought we to pray for those who are grieving?

  If you are in a group, have the members discuss times when they have been ministered to by others or have ministered to others during times of grief. Ask: What was said or done that was especially meaningful during these times?

PRAYER

Commit what you have learned from God's Word in this lesson to prayer.

- Praise God that He is the One true and *living* God who raises from the dead.
- Confess any frustration you have felt on account of the death of a loved one that was in accordance with our call to self-denial.
- Thank God for preparing you to minister to others with the truth of the gospel, having been intimately acquainted with its reality yourself.
- Ask God to help you to further prepare yourself by actively thinking about what it will mean to minister to someone who is dying or grieving.

REVIEW QUIZ

Use these multiple-choice questions to measure what you learned from this lesson.

1. What is *not* one of the five ideas to help you minister to those who are dying?
   a. Pray
   b. Prepare
   c. Prognosis
   d. Prolong
2. We might be tempted to provide solutions to people who are dying and feel the weight of this pressure, but often our presence is all that is needed for them.
   a. True
   b. False
3. What aspect of God's will was specifically named as relating to our time of death?
   a. Decretive will
   b. Preceptive will
   c. Revealed will
   d. Secret will
4. Whose daughter said, "Yes, dearest Father, as God wills," when facing death?
   a. John Calvin
   b. John Owen
   c. Martin Luther
   d. Samuel Rutherford
5. It is not sinful to yield to God's providence if it is believed that nothing can prevent an imminent death.
   a. True
   b. False

6. Which of the following is *not* one of the three ideas to help you minister to those who are grieving?
   a. Serve
   b. Speak
   c. Step in
   d. Stir up

Answer Key—How Do I Help the Dying & Grieving?

REFLECTION & DISCUSSION QUESTIONS

Before the Video

What Do You Think?

These are personal questions. The answers should be based on your own knowledge and experience.

Scripture Reading

- How might this passage about the comfort that God gives us in affliction also be applied to ministering to those who are dying or grieving?

  God is the God of all *comfort. The comfort that He supplies to us in times of affliction through persecution also extends to the trials that accompany death. Just as we have been comforted by the gospel and rest in the God who raises the dead, so also we ought to give others this message of hope in the face of death. Paul teaches us that in life and in death we must rely on God. Calling those who are dying or those who are grieving to this reliance is a great blessing to the Christian.*

During the Video

Ministering Well

- What is the best way to prepare ourselves to minister to someone who is dying?

  To prepare ourselves to minister to someone who is dying, we must equip ourselves with Scripture that deals with life-and-death realities. In this way, we ready ourselves to address how the gospel deals with these realities. We also do well to prepare ourselves concerning the condition of the person whom we may be visiting. We must be prepared to see our loved ones after they have undergone significant physical changes while remembering that though they may be decaying physically, they are very much alive spiritually in Christ.

- What is often required in our bearing the burdens of others, even while remaining silent in the face of their suffering?

  It is hard to bear another's burdens without trying to fix everything. Often, all that is required of us is to be present with the dying while remaining silent. This, however, requires self-denial. It is not pleasant, but being present with someone as a way of bearing his or her burden is an act of love.

- What passage in the Bible might cause someone difficulty in accepting a physician's prognosis that death is quickly approaching for someone?

James 5:15 says, "And the prayer of faith will save the one who is sick, and the Lord will raise him up." This verse contains a wonderful promise, but it may be challenging to us when we hear a dire prognosis. Though we ought to pray, it should not assail our faith if, in the Lord's providence, death should come.

Pointing, Praying, Serving, Speaking

- What is a good way to open up gospel conversations with someone who is about to die? What are some examples of this?

  One suggestion was to ask open-ended questions in order to broach the subject of eternal realities. We might ask questions such as these: What are you thinking about? Do you have any fears or worries? Is there anything you'd like to say while I'm here? Asking such questions may give us a great opportunity to share the gospel with an unbeliever and to reassure a believer.

- What three things ought we to do for those who are grieving the death of a loved one?

  When someone is grieving, we can look for ways to step into the person's life and serve him or her in an unobtrusive manner, such as making meals or hosting people who are in town for the funeral. But a person's grief does not end after the funeral is over, and this is why we must serve for the long haul. Finally, we should not feel strange in speaking about a deceased loved one to a person who is mourning. It is an opportunity to share how the deceased touched the lives of others, especially if it was for Christ and His kingdom.

After the Video

- Which of the five principles for ministering to those who are dying do you find to be most helpful at this time and why?

  Answers to this question will vary but should explain why one of the following five principles for ministering to those who are dying was particularly helpful to you: prepare, presence, prognosis, point, and pray.

- How would you respond to someone who could not accept the coming death of a loved one on account of his or her understanding of James 5:15?

  James 5:15 calls us to great faith, but it might also make us think that we are being faithless to respect a physician's prognosis that death is certain and near. If we consider the context of James' letter, we can protect ourselves from feeling this way. James 4 uses the phrase "if the Lord wills" in regard to our being presumptuous about our plans (v. 15). It just may be the case that the Lord has willed our loved one's death, and a severe prognosis may be indicating that reality. James even says that our life is "a mist that appears for a little time and then vanishes" (v. 14). Furthermore, James' letter started with the truth that Christians are not spared from trials and so are also not spared from the trials that accompany death. James also points to examples such as Job and Elijah to teach us steadfastness and faithfulness in prayer. So we ought to pray, but we can be assured that God will ultimately answer the promise of James 5:15 at the resurrection. In this sense, God does heal every Christian, even from death, but He has not promised this universally in this life.

- What types of prayers were commended in this lecture for those who are dying? What types of prayers ought we to pray for those who are grieving?

  The second question requires you to consider the types of prayers that we ought to pray for the grieving and can be wide-ranging depending on someone's circumstances. Here are some of the examples that Dr. Waters gave for what we can be praying for those who are in the process of dying: that they would have a sure and settled faith in Jesus Christ, that they would submit themselves to the will of God, that they would have comfort of body and soul, that the Lord would take them quickly, and that the Lord would make provision for the loved ones they leave behind.

REVIEW QUIZ

1. **D.**
   Each of these single words was used alliteratively to help you memorize ways that you can minister well to those who are dying except prolong. *The ideas connoted by the word* prolong *push back against such measures to effective ministry as being present with someone, honoring someone's prognosis, and how we might pray for someone who is dying.*

2. **A.**
   Sometimes we can do more damage than good when we feel the need to fix everything for the person who is nearing death. We run the risk of being like Job's friends, who would have been wise to remain silent. Ministering to someone who is about to die does not mean that we need to have all the right words, but our presence can still bring great comfort.

3. **D.**
   Distinctions can be made concerning the will of God, though God is not divided in His will. Dr. Waters identified God's "secret will" specifically in relation to the time of our deaths. This is not something that we can know. God's decretive will relates to His eternal decree of all things that come to pass, so it is also a correct answer, though this term was not used by Dr. Waters.

4. **C.**
   Each of these theologians lived to see the untimely deaths of their children. John Owen suffered the loss of ten children in infancy. It was Martin Luther's daughter Magdalena, however, who said, "Yes, dearest Father, as God wills," when asked

whether she would gladly go to be with the heavenly Father though leaving her earthly father behind.

5. **A.**
   We ought to pray for someone's healing, but we also do not need to consider it sinful to respect a physician's prognosis concerning the health of a loved one who is about to die. In respecting a physician's prognosis, we also respect our loved one, who is aware that God's providence has brought death near.

6. **D.**
   Though we may be able to "stir up" someone's affections for a departed loved one, Dr. Waters recommended that the way to do this is to "speak" to the person of the deceased. This may seem counterintuitive when compared to our stepping in to help and serving for the long haul, but actually speaking about how much someone who has died meant to us, when done in a sensitive manner, can bring a person who is grieving to delightfully remember him or her.

8

How Do I Prepare for Death? Spiritual Preparations

INTRODUCTION

We have a privilege as Christians of ministering to others who are dying and grieving because we have a biblical concept of what death is and the comfort that we have in the gospel. But we must still prepare for death ourselves. The first main category of our preparation for death is spiritual. In this lesson, Dr. Waters provides five ways in which we must prepare ourselves individually for death.

LEARNING GOALS

When you have finished this lesson, you should be able to:

- Define five things to prepare yourself for death spiritually
- Articulate practical ways of living out these five preparations day to day
- Understand how you are to think about yourself as a believer in relation to the world

KEY IDEAS

- Living the Christian life well is the best way to prepare for death.
- We need the ministry of the Word to keep us spiritually well and healthy in the Christian life.
- We must cling to Christ in this life, recognizing that we are passing through this world as pilgrims to a heavenly home.

REFLECTION & DISCUSSION QUESTIONS

Before the Video

What Do You Think?

Take a moment to answer the following questions. They will prepare you for the lecture.

- Are you spiritually prepared to die? In what way?

- What do you fear losing most in this world? What do you long for most in heaven?

Scripture Reading

If then you have been raised with Christ, seek the things that are above, where Christ is, seated at the right hand of God. Set your minds on things that are above, not on things that are on earth. For you have died, and your life is hidden with Christ in God. When Christ who is your life appears, then you also will appear with him in glory. Put to death therefore what is earthly in you.

—Colossians 3:1–5a

- What is the major contrast in this passage? How are we encouraged to live in light of this contrast?

During the Video

Answer the following questions while you watch the video. They will guide you through the lecture.

Our Vital Need *0:00–14:05*

- What is the first thing that we should be doing to prepare for death? What happens if we neglect doing this?

- What is the second thing that we must do to prepare for death? How is this described in Scripture?

Our Heavenly Hope *14:05–24:16*

- What is our "ministry" to other Christians?

- What are some of the connotations of the way that "world" is used in the Bible?

- Since we are called to hold loosely to the world, where should we direct our minds?

After the Video

Answer the following questions after you have finished the lecture. They will help you identify and summarize the major points.

- How are we to live day by day in communion with Christ and the Spirit? Can you think of any ways to practically facilitate this in your life?

  If you are in a group, have the members read Romans 8:1–11 and compare it with Colossians 3:1–17.

- What does our relationship with the Holy Spirit have to do with death and our preparing to die?

  If you are in a group, have the members discuss whether they think ideas such as communion with Christ and life in the Spirit sound mysterious. Ask: In what ways did Dr. Waters help you to see that these concepts are not so mysterious if understood in terms of our daily walk as Christians?

- Of the five things that believers ought to be doing to ready themselves for death, which do you need to cultivate the most? How will you go about doing this?

  If you are in a group, have the members discuss ways that the church connects to and is a core way of living out these five means of preparing to die spiritually.

PRAYER

Commit what you have learned from God's Word in this lesson to prayer.

- Praise God that His kingdom is one that cannot be shaken.
- Confess times when you hold too tightly to the things of the world as if they were ultimate.
- Thank God for the Holy Spirit, who was given to you and enables you to walk in faithful obedience as a pilgrim disciple of Christ.
- Ask God to help you think more deeply on the reality of your citizenship in heaven.

REVIEW QUIZ

Use these multiple-choice questions to measure what you learned from this lesson.

1. Which of the following is *not* one of the five things that we ought to be doing to prepare for death spiritually?
   a. Thinking often of heaven
   b. Praying more to the Father
   c. Holding the world loosely
   d. Enjoying fellowship with God's people

2. The Lord's Day most connects to which of the five things that we ought to be doing to prepare for death spiritually?
   a. Thinking often of heaven
   b. Holding the world loosely
   c. Communing often with Christ
   d. Attending to the means of grace

3. If one is able to go but neglects going to church, which of the following things that we ought to be doing to prepare for death spiritually is also most likely being neglected?
   a. Thinking often of heaven
   b. Holding the world loosely
   c. Enjoying fellowship with God's people
   d. Communing often with Christ

4. The entire Christian life is a preparation for death.
   a. True
   b. False

5. Since there remains a goodness about the world, we must hold tightly to this goodness.
   a. True
   b. False

6. What word did Dr. Waters use to describe what God did *not* design the world to be?
   a. Fallen
   b. Home
   c. Permanent
   d. Satisfying

Answer Key—How Do I Prepare for Death?

Spiritual Preparations

REFLECTION & DISCUSSION QUESTIONS

Before the Video

What Do You Think?

These are personal questions. The answers should be based on your own knowledge and experience.

Scripture Reading

- What is the major contrast in this passage? How are we encouraged to live in light of this contrast?

  The major contrast in this passage is between the things that are above and things that are below, between the heavenly and the earthly. United to Christ, our lives are hidden with Him in heaven even now such that, in Him, we have already died. For this reason, we are called to set our minds on heavenly things and put to death what is earthly in us. See the remainder of Colossians 3:5–17 for practical ways that Paul gives us to live this out.

During the Video

Our Vital Need

- What is the first thing that we should be doing to prepare for death? What happens if we neglect doing this?

  The first thing that we should be doing is attending to the means of grace. Fundamentally, this means going to church and worshiping God, for there we encounter His ordinary means of grace through His Word. In worship we regularly hear the gospel and so are reminded of our certain hope of eternal life. If we are not hearing God's Word in worship, then we will become spiritually anemic. Just as we need a regular diet of healthy food to eat, so we need a regular diet of the ministry of the Word of God to keep us spiritually well and healthy, grounding us in our heavenly hope.

- What is the second thing that we must do to prepare for death? How is this described in Scripture?

  The second thing that we must do to prepare for death is communing often with Christ. As Christians, we are united to Christ and are to live in Him. This is what Paul describes in Galatians 2 when he says: "I have been crucified with Christ.

It is no longer I who live, but Christ who lives in me. And the life I now live in the flesh I live by faith in the Son of God, who loved me and gave himself for me" (v. 20). For Paul, "to live is Christ" (Phil. 1:21). In our union with Christ, His death and resurrection life are ours.

Our Heavenly Hope

- What is our "ministry" to other Christians?

  Our ministry to other Christians is a "ministry of provocation." This does not mean that we are to irritate one another but that we are to stir one another up to love and good works (see Heb. 10:24). This is not possible if we are not gathering together as a church and fellowshipping with one another as believers.

- What are some of the connotations of the way that "world" is used in the Bible?

  "World" can mean various things when used in the Bible. Often it can carry a sense of humanity's rebellion against God. Sometimes it can refer more generally to God's good creation. Yet while the world remains God's good creation despite the fall, we must regard ourselves as strangers in it.

- Since we are called to hold loosely to the world, where should we direct our minds?

  We are pilgrims in this world, and one of the ways to prepare for our departure from this world is to hold on to the things of this world loosely. We can also direct our minds toward heaven. We are citizens of heaven (Phil. 3:20), and while we are in this world, thinking often of heaven can only increase our longing for home and ready us for death.

After the Video

- How are we to live day by day in communion with Christ and the Spirit? Can you think of any ways to practically facilitate this in your life?

  The realities of our union with Christ may seem more concrete than what it means to commune with Him. But just as we are united to Christ by faith, so we commune with Him by faith. We dwell on the realities of our union as a way of fellowshipping with Him, and He also indwells us by the Holy Spirit. We can live a lifestyle in keeping with Christ and the Spirit by doing what is pleasing to the Spirit, which is being obedient to the Word of God.

- What does our relationship with the Holy Spirit have to do with death and our preparing to die?

  Our obedience to God is evidence of the Spirit's indwelling and our true communion with Christ and His death and resurrection. In the Christian life, the Spirit makes Himself known to us by changing us from the inside through our sanctification. We have been brought to life through Him, and though we die and our bodies decay on the outside, we are very much alive inwardly. Our inner renewal by the

Spirit will even be one day matched by our outer renewal through the resurrection: "If the Spirit of him who raised Jesus from the dead dwells in you, he who raised Christ Jesus from the dead will also give life to your mortal bodies through his Spirit who dwells in you" (Rom. 8:11).

- Of the five things that believers ought to be doing to ready themselves for death, which do you need to cultivate the most? How will you go about doing this?

  Answers to these questions will vary and are personal in nature. The five things that we ought to be doing to ready ourselves for death are attending to the means of grace, communing often with Christ, fellowshipping with God's people, holding this world loosely, and thinking often of heaven.

REVIEW QUIZ

1. **B.**
   While prayer is one of the ways that we commune with God and is a means of grace that we have the privilege of enjoying in worship, and is thus subsumed under many of the five things that we ought to be doing to prepare for death spiritually, it is not one of the five things itself.

2. **D.**
   God calls us to worship on the Lord's Day, and in worship we are able to attend to the means of grace, so the Lord's Day is most closely associated to attending to the means of grace, though it is a true expression and means of communing with Christ on His day.

3. **C.**
   If one is not gathering to worship, it is most likely that fellowshipping with God's people is also being neglected. Though each of these may connect to worship in a real sense, it is most difficult to conceive of how such fellowship is possible and sustained apart from worship.

4. **A.**
   To prepare ourselves spiritually for death is not something to which we should give only a few weeks or months. It is not even something that we reserve for later years in our lives. It is something that we prepare for our whole lives.

5. **B.**
   The Bible can be referring to the world in the sense of its being God's good creation, and despite the fall, this world remains good and is God's world. Yet even with the good things that we enjoy in this world, we are to consider ourselves strangers and exiles in it.

6. **C.**
   One of the ways that we can hold loosely to the world and think of heaven more often is to remember that the world is not permanent. God never designed the world that we experience to be permanent. As we look to heavenly realities in preparation for death, it is good to remind ourselves that God's kingdom, unlike the world, will never pass away or be shaken.

9

How Do I Prepare for Death? This-Worldly Preparations

INTRODUCTION

In addition to preparing ourselves spiritually for death, we must also put many worldly things in order for the sake of our loved ones. While this might seem unspiritual in comparison with our spiritual preparations to stand confidently in Christ before our Maker, "this-worldly" preparations are far from being unspiritual. In this lesson, Dr. Waters provides practical steps to prepare our worldly affairs before death.

LEARNING GOALS

When you have finished this lesson, you should be able to:

- Explain this-worldly preparations for death in four areas
- Provide biblical support for the wisdom of making these preparations
- Name various tips and principles in making this-worldly preparations

KEY IDEAS

- We ought to prepare our families, our worldly estates, our end-of-life wishes, and our funerals and burials in the event of our deaths.
- This-worldly preparations are matters that testify of our faith in Jesus Christ and can point others to Him.
- Speaking with our families about our deaths and ordering our worldly affairs ought to be done in a timely manner, and seeking reconciliation if needed ought to be done now.

REFLECTION & DISCUSSION QUESTIONS

Before the Video

What Do You Think?

Take a moment to answer the following questions. They will prepare you for the lecture.

- Have you ever considered all that goes into preparing to die? Do you have any wishes for what happens to your possessions or at your funeral, for example, that need to be communicated?

- Have you ever experienced or had family members who experienced the death of a loved one and all that went into processing the person's estate? Had things been put in order before the person died?

Scripture Reading

I did not say these things to you from the beginning, because I was with you. But now I am going to him who sent me, and none of you asks me, "Where are you going?" But because I have said these things to you, sorrow has filled your heart. Nevertheless, I tell you the truth: it is to your advantage that I go away, for if I do not go away, the Helper will not come to you. But if I go, I will send him to you.

—John 16:4b–7

- Jesus prepared His disciples for His death. How does this idea inform our own preparations? How did Jesus encourage His disciples?

During the Video

Answer the following questions while you watch the video. They will guide you through the lecture.

Preparing Our Families and Ordering Our Estates *0:00–11:12*

- What does Scripture give as a clear pattern that can be applied to preparing our families before we die? What are some examples?

- What three themes are a part of this scriptural pattern?

- What is the best thing to do to prepare our worldly estates?

Preparing for End of Life and after Death *11:12–22:44*

- What is the starting framework for our end-of-life decisions? How does the Westminster Shorter Catechism show its relevance to these matters?

- What three principles must we consider in making end-of-life decisions and plans?

- What is the ultimate aim for all our planning?

After the Video

Answer the following questions after you have finished the lecture. They will help you identify and summarize the major points.

- Which of the three themes found in farewell addresses in the Bible is most striking to you and why? Has someone ever given you a farewell like this? If so, describe what was said. Is this something important for you to do? Why or why not?

  If you are in a group, have the members read Acts 20:17–38. Ask: Where are these three themes found in Paul's farewell? What is striking about what Paul emphasizes or his emotions?

- What are some practical ways in which you could communicate something approximating the farewell addresses in the Bible with your loved ones? Are these parting words suitable for reconciliation? Why or why not?

  If you are in a group, have the members recall what Paul said in Romans 12: "If possible, so far as it depends on you, live peaceably with all" (v. 18). Ask: Why should we as Christians strive for reconciliation? What are examples of situations in which reconciliation is outside our control?

- Our personal preparation for death is a way of loving our neighbors. In what ways do you think the four areas of our preparation are particularly acts of love?

  If you are in a group, have the members share their own experiences in dealing with someone's estate or significant end-of-life decisions. Try to pinpoint the different experiences of those who were left with a well-ordered estate and those who were not.

PRAYER

Commit what you have learned from God's Word in this lesson to prayer.

- Praise God for His wisdom, which knows no end.
- Confess ways that you have been hard-hearted in seeking reconciliation with those you have sinned against or who have sinned against you.
- Thank God that the application of biblical principles to what may seem like worldly cares is extremely practical and spiritual.
- Ask God to help you take steps toward loving others in preparing for your death.

REVIEW QUIZ

Use these multiple-choice questions to measure what you learned from this lesson.

1. Which of the following books of the Bible was called a farewell address in itself?
   a. Numbers
   b. Deuteronomy
   c. Acts
   d. Revelation

2. Scripture commands us to formulate farewell addresses for our loved ones.
   a. True
   b. False

3. Which of the following preparations is best handled in an official and legal manner?
   a. Farewell addresses
   b. Funeral and burial wishes
   c. End-of-life decisions
   d. All of the above

4. Which of the following is *not* one of the three principles for making end-of-life decisions?
   a. The goal of medicine
   b. The inevitability of death
   c. The morality of unjust killing
   d. The preferred place of our possessions

5. The practice of burying the dead has scriptural and historical weight behind it.
   a. True
   b. False

6. What one word can summarize the end for all our preparations for our deaths?
   a. Wisdom
   b. Love
   c. Heaven
   d. Glory

Answer Key—How Do I Prepare for Death? This-Worldly Preparations

REFLECTION & DISCUSSION QUESTIONS

Before the Video

What Do You Think?

These are personal questions. The answers should be based on your own knowledge and experience.

Scripture Reading

- Jesus prepared His disciples for His death. How does this idea inform our own preparations? How did Jesus encourage His disciples?

  Jesus prepared His disciples for His death, giving us an example of a good way of preparing our loved ones for our own deaths. In the upper room, Jesus pointed His disciples to and encouraged them with a promise, and while we cannot promise the same type of thing, we can point our dear ones to Him.

During the Video

Preparing Our Families and Ordering Our Estates

- What does Scripture give as a clear pattern that can be applied to preparing our families before we die? What are some examples?

  From Genesis into the books of the New Testament, we observe a pattern of farewell addresses. While not commanded in Scripture, this pattern is given to us by way of example. Some examples are Jacob's farewell to his sons, Moses' farewell to Israel, David's farewell to Solomon, Jesus' farewell to His disciples, and Paul's farewell to the elders at Ephesus.

- What three themes are a part of this scriptural pattern?

  The many farewell addresses in Scripture seek to remind others of God's faithfulness, point them to His promises, and call them to fellowship with Him. These three themes can richly inform how we speak to others as we approach death.

- What is the best thing to do to prepare our worldly estates?

  While we are in good health, mentally and physically, the best thing that we can do to prepare our worldly estates is to craft an "appropriate, comprehensive, and legal plan" that ensures that our money and worldly possessions go precisely to whom we want them to go.

Preparing for End of Life and after Death

- What is the starting framework for our end-of-life decisions? How does the Westminster Shorter Catechism show its relevance to these matters?

  God's law is the starting framework for making end-of-life decisions. The Westminster Shorter Catechism gives an exposition of the Ten Commandments and provides positive requirements for keeping these commandments. For the sixth commandment, which tells us that unjustly taking another's life is a violation of God's law, the positive dimension of that law is our duty also to preserve our own lives and the lives of others, which connects directly to all our end-of-life decisions.

- What three principles must we consider in making end-of-life decisions and plans?

  The first principle is that unjust killing is always wrong. The practice of euthanasia as an act of intentionally bringing someone's life to an end is sinful. The second principle is that the goal of medicine is to bring a person from sickness to health. Understanding this goal can help us weigh the benefits of a certain treatment. The third principle is that death is inevitable. Whereas hastening the death of another violates the sixth commandment, we can in good conscience refuse some interventions that may do more harm than good and pursue a course of treatment that allows us to live our remaining days in a dignified and comfortable way.

- What is the ultimate aim for all our planning?

  When we plan properly in advance for our deaths, we are demonstrating love for those who are around us. It is a fulfillment of the second table of the law, which can help point others away from us and to the love of God in Jesus Christ.

After the Video

- Which of the three themes found in farewell addresses in the Bible is most striking to you and why? Has someone ever given you a farewell like this? If so, describe what was said. Is this something important for you to do? Why or why not?

  Answers to this question may vary but should identify one theme found within the farewell addresses in the Bible as outstanding. The three common features are reminding others of God's faithfulness, pointing them to His promises, and calling them to fellowship with Him. If our primary purpose in ordering our affairs before death is love, then making this type of farewell address to our loved ones should be something that we prioritize.

- What are some practical ways in which you could communicate something approximating the farewell addresses in the Bible with your loved ones? Are these parting words suitable for reconciliation? Why or why not?

  The examples of farewell addresses in the Bible are varied in terms of their circumstances. Some are intimate, while others are addressed to a large audience. As we consider how best to approach communicating this type of farewell personally, we must remember that we have freedom. We don't have to address a large group of people at once, and we can even write letters to others. Furthermore, we can even do this before our final hours. As for reconciliation, if such an occasion is our only opportunity, then we must take it. Dr. Waters did emphasize, however, that reconciliation isn't to be saved for the end of life. For Christians, keeping short accounts is something to do throughout one's life.

- Our personal preparation for death is a way of loving our neighbors. In what ways do you think the four areas of our preparation are particularly acts of love?

  Answers may vary in identifying what is loving about each of the four areas of our preparation. Here are some examples: When we give a farewell address to our loved ones in line with the patterns that the Bible provides, we assure them of God's faithfulness to us, His promises to them, and the importance of greater fellowship with Him. Each of these is an expression of love to those whom we leave behind to grieve our deaths. When our desires for our worldly possessions are made clear, we prevent strife from arising over our possessions while we provide for our loved ones. When our instructions for end-of-life care are explicit, then we might ease the consciences of those who have to make hard decisions for us. Finally, when our funerals and burials are planned, we take the guesswork away concerning our wishes.

REVIEW QUIZ

1. **B.**
   Dr. Waters called the whole of Deuteronomy a farewell address from Moses to Israel. Paul's final letter to Timothy, too, can be considered a farewell address from a spiritual father to his child.

2. **B.**
   Scripture contains no command to give a farewell address. In many of the circumstances in life, this is not possible. But Scripture does contain many farewell addresses, showing that such addresses are a regular pattern and a natural part of human life.

3. **C.**
   We ought to be clear about making our wishes known to our loved ones, both in what we wish to communicate to them in our final words and in what we would like for our funerals and burials. While these should be clear, they do not require the weight of law. Empowering the right person to make end-of-life decisions on our behalf, however, does require that we legally establish a durable power of attorney.

4. **D.**
   End-of-life care has to do with the critical decisions that need to be made before

our deaths when we cannot make such decisions for ourselves. Though designating where we would like our possessions to go in the event of our deaths is one of the main areas of our preparations for death, it does not directly connect to end-of-life decisions.

5. **A.**
Dr. Waters maintains that the decision to bury or cremate a loved one is not an issue of conscience. In other words, it is not a sin if one decides to cremate or bury. But the witness of Scripture and the historical practice of Christians do indicate a preference for burial as a powerful anticipation of the resurrection of the body.

6. **B.**
Preparing for our deaths is wise. Preparing for our deaths is also unto God's glory and, for Christians, charged with the hope of heaven. But the one thing that was emphasized for why we prepare our worldly affairs for others in the event of our deaths is love.

10

What Does the Bible Teach about the Resurrection?

INTRODUCTION

With all that we must know about death and all that we must do to prepare for it in this life, it is ultimately what comes after death that informs what we think and what we do. The last three lectures of this series cover the biblical teaching about what comes after death. In this lesson, Dr. Waters walks us through the *locus classicus* on the significance of the resurrection for believers in Scripture: Paul's defense of Christ's resurrection and our resurrection in 1 Corinthians 15.

LEARNING GOALS

When you have finished this lesson, you should be able to:

- Summarize the teaching of 1 Corinthians 15
- Articulate why the resurrection is integral to the gospel
- Identify the contrasts that Paul makes between our bodies in Adam and our resurrection bodies in Christ

KEY IDEAS

- The resurrection is not peripheral to the gospel but is so essential to it that if it were denied, there would be no Christian hope for salvation.
- The bodily resurrection of believers and the bodily resurrection of Christ are inseparable.
- Our future resurrections give meaning to the present.

REFLECTION & DISCUSSION QUESTIONS

Before the Video

What Do You Think?

Take a moment to answer the following questions. They will prepare you for the lecture.

- Do you tend to view your body as something positive or negative? Why?

- What major questions do you have about the resurrection body?

Scripture Reading

Brothers, join in imitating me, and keep your eyes on those who walk according to the example you have in us. For many, of whom I have often told you and now tell you even with tears, walk as enemies of the cross of Christ. Their end is destruction, their god is their belly, and they glory in their shame, with minds set on earthly things. But our citizenship is in heaven, and from it we await a Savior, the Lord Jesus Christ, who will transform our lowly body to be like his glorious body, by the power that enables him even to subject all things to himself.

—Philippians 3:17–21

- What are the two contrasting "glories" of believers and the enemies of Christ whom Paul is describing?

During the Video

Answer the following questions while you watch the video. They will guide you through the lecture.

At the Heart of the Gospel *0:00–11:00*

- What is significant about the word "delivered" in the first section of 1 Corinthians 15? What was "delivered"?

- Why are our resurrections guaranteed or inseparable from Christ's resurrection?

The Resurrection Body *11:00–23:39*

- What are some key contrasting terms about our bodies in the third section of 1 Corinthians 15?

- What can we infer about the resurrected bodies of the wicked from Paul's teaching?

After the Video

Answer the following questions after you have finished the lecture. They will help you identify and summarize the major points.

- What would be the case if Christ had not been raised? Since He has been raised, what are the implications of His resurrection?

  If you are in a group, have the members read Acts 17:22–34. Ask: Where is scorn shown for Paul's teaching? What does Paul teach that the resurrection means for all people?

- What is the difference between our bodies "in Adam" and our resurrection bodies "in Christ"? Of all the ways that Paul describes the resurrection body, what makes you most hopeful for the resurrection?

  If you are in a group, have the members discuss what they think about the resurrection body after hearing this lecture. Ask: What questions do you still have for which Scripture perhaps does not provide answers? How do the answers that Scripture provides for other questions make you certain in your faith nonetheless?

- What should reflection on our future resurrected bodies bring about in this life? What did it bring about for Paul? To what does he call us?

  If you are in a group, have the members discuss how reflecting on their identity in Christ can affect their daily interactions with others and with themselves. Ask: How does your new identity in Christ teach you to deal with personal conflict or guilt and shame?

PRAYER

Commit what you have learned from God's Word in this lesson to prayer.

- Praise God—Father, Son, and Holy Spirit—for the power on display at Christ's resurrection.

- Confess any ways that you dishonor your body despite the hope of the resurrection.
- Thank God for the guarantee that He has given to us in the resurrection of His Son.
- Ask God to enable you to witness concerning the certainty of the resurrection to those whom you long to see resurrected to eternal life and not to eternal destruction.

REVIEW QUIZ

Use these multiple-choice questions to measure what you learned from this lesson.

1. What is *not* one of the words that summarize the four sections of 1 Corinthians 15?
   a. Delivered
   b. How
   c. That
   d. Why

2. Paul declares the gospel in 1 Corinthians 15 without concern for proofs of Christ's death and resurrection because of the gospel's power.
   a. True
   b. False

3. What key word guarantees our resurrections?
   a. Power
   b. Imperishable
   c. Glorious
   d. Firstfruits

4. What is the contrast between our "natural" bodies and our "spiritual" bodies?
   a. The body outside and the body inside
   b. The physical and spiritual bodies of the resurrection
   c. The body in Adam and the resurrected body in Christ
   d. The present physical body and the nonphysical body of the resurrection

5. Scripture teaches but doesn't often reflect on the resurrection of the wicked.
   a. True
   b. False

6. Why does Paul call the resurrection bodies of believers "glorious"?
   a. The nature of all resurrection bodies is glorious.
   b. Where we will be in heaven is often described as our being in "glory."
   c. Christ's resurrection body is glorious, just as ours will be.
   d. Our resurrection bodies will be glorious to behold.

Answer Key—What Does the Bible Teach about the Resurrection?

REFLECTION & DISCUSSION QUESTIONS

Before the Video

What Do You Think?

These are personal questions. The answers should be based on your own knowledge and experience.

Scripture Reading

- What are the two contrasting "glories" of believers and the enemies of Christ whom Paul is describing?

  This passage encourages us to be steadfast in righteousness. Those who walk as enemies of Christ are described as glorying in their shame—that which ought to be the source of shame is something that they boast in. This is somehow connected to their relationship with their bodies, their god being "their belly." Though the bodies of believers are described in opposite terms, as "lowly" in the following verses, they will be transformed by Christ into glorious bodies.

During the Video

At the Heart of the Gospel

- What is significant about the word "delivered" in the first section of 1 Corinthians 15? What was "delivered"?

  Paul writes to the Corinthians about the gospel that was "delivered" to them and that they "received" (1 Cor. 15:1, 3) before teaching about the resurrection of Christ. Christ's death and resurrection were central to Paul's teaching—at its very heart. As something "delivered," the resurrection's place in the gospel is not optional. If it is lost, then the gospel that was delivered is lost.

- Why are our resurrections guaranteed or inseparable from Christ's resurrection?

  The bodily resurrections of believers and the resurrection of Christ are inseparable because we are united to Christ. He is the firstfruits of the resurrection. Just as the firstfruits of a harvest guarantee the harvest to come, so Christ's resurrection guarantees our resurrections.

The Resurrection Body

- What are some key contrasting terms about our bodies in the third section of

1 Corinthians 15?

Paul contrasts the resurrection body with the state of our bodies as they are now (see 1 Cor. 15:42–49). Our bodies now are perishable; the resurrection body will be imperishable. Our bodies now are dishonored by sin; the resurrection body will be glorious. Our bodies now are weak; the resurrection body will be raised in power. Finally, our bodies are, "in Adam," natural; the resurrection body "in Christ" is spiritually alive.

- What can we infer about the resurrected bodies of the wicked from Paul's teaching?

  Scripture does not often reflect on the resurrection of the wicked and what their resurrected bodies will be like. If the resurrection bodies of the righteous in Christ are imperishable, glorious, powerful, and spiritually alive, it may be inferred that the resurrection bodies of the wicked are the opposite. They will be things not of glory but of shame, contemptible and suited to eternal judgment.

After the Video

- What would be the case if Christ had not been raised? Since He has been raised, what are the implications of His resurrection?

  Paul confronted the teaching of some in the Corinthian church for denying a bodily resurrection. Paul shows that the denial of our bodily resurrections has certain implications, especially as relating to the resurrection of Christ, since the two are tied together. If Christ had not been raised, Paul argues, then the Apostles would have been teaching falsehood and whatever faith believers had would have been founded on falsehood. Further, if it were the case that Jesus had not been raised, then we would all still be dead in our sins and will perish. For the Corinthians, a denial of our bodily resurrections attacked Christ's resurrection. But Jesus has been raised, winning complete victory of sin, death, and the grave and right now ruling and reigning over all things.

- What is the difference between our bodies "in Adam" and our resurrection bodies "in Christ"? Of all the ways that Paul describes the resurrection body, what makes you most hopeful for the resurrection?

  Our bodies because of sin are perishable, weak, and dishonored by sin, but our resurrection bodies made after the image of Christ will be imperishable, raised in power, and glorious. Paul's description of the resurrection body in 1 Corinthians 15 should make us await this aspect of our redemption eagerly. Answers to the second question are subjective and take your personal experience into consideration. If you have struggled with sickness and pain or a deep hatred of your sin, one of Paul's descriptions of the resurrection body may have stuck out to you more than others.

- What should reflection on our future resurrected bodies bring about in this life?

What did it bring about for Paul? To what does he call us?

In Paul's defense of the reality of the bodily resurrection and Christ's resurrection, he considers his own suffering and the suffering of fellow believers who are "in danger every hour" on account of the gospel (1 Cor. 15:30). Paul and other Christians suffer for Christ, and His resurrection gives that suffering meaning. At the end of 1 Corinthians 15 and because our future resurrections give meaning to the present, Paul also calls the Corinthians to deeper faith: "Therefore, my beloved brothers, be steadfast, immovable, always abounding in the work of the Lord, knowing that in the Lord your labor is not in vain" (v. 58). Our present life in the body is to be lived in this hope, and knowing that our bodies will one day be raised, we ought to honor them and glorify God in them.

REVIEW QUIZ

1. **D.**
   In 1 Corinthians 15, Paul does provide an answer for why the resurrection occurred, but why *was not one of the key words that Dr. Waters drew out for our understanding of Paul's teaching in the four sections of this chapter. Those words were* delivered, that, how, *and* victory.

2. **A.**
   The gospel is powerful. It is the power of God for salvation (see Rom. 1:16). But the gospel's power does not mean that it can't be adorned with reasons to believe it. In Paul's teaching about what the gospel is, he points to two proofs for the death and resurrection of Christ, both that He "was buried" and that Christ appeared bodily to many after that.

3. **D.**
   Most of these words describe the resurrection body, but one ought to stand out to you concerning how your resurrection connects with Christ's resurrection. His resurrection guarantees your resurrection because He is the firstfruits of this harvest (see 1 Cor. 15:20–22).

4. **C.**
   When Paul identifies our resurrected bodies as spiritual, he does not mean that they will be nonphysical. They will, however, be like Christ's resurrected body, for believers are united to Him and will experience a resurrection like His. Just as He was raised physically, so we will be raised spiritually. Paul's distinction needs to be understood in terms of the body "in Adam" and the body "in Christ."

5. **A.**
   While Scripture speaks about the resurrection of believers and all other people in no uncertain terms, there are not many descriptions about the resurrection of the wicked like what we get concerning the righteous in 1 Corinthians 15. Dr. Waters

pointed to Paul's speech before Felix in Acts 24 as one instance among others in which we learn about the resurrection of the wicked.

6. **D.**
The wicked will not be raised in glorious resurrection bodies; not all resurrection bodies will be glorious. Believers, however, will experience the resurrection in the same manner as Christ experienced the resurrection. Our resurrection bodies will be like His—glorious.

11

What Does the Bible Teach about the Final Judgment?

INTRODUCTION

What we do with our lives and whom we place our faith in matters. The author of Hebrews tells us, "It is appointed for man to die once, and after that comes judgment" (9:27). This judgment that comes immediately upon death is followed by a final judgment after the resurrection of the body. In this lesson, Dr. Waters answers key questions about the nature of the final judgment while connecting it to the gospel and the reasons that believers can look forward to that day.

LEARNING GOALS

When you have finished this lesson, you should be able to:

- Distinguish between types of judgment and their outcomes
- Describe what the final judgment will be like according to Scripture
- Articulate the gospel as it relates to the final judgment

KEY IDEAS

- To remove the final judgment from the gospel is to gut the work of Christ of its meaning.
- The final judgment will be just, true, final, and beyond appeal.
- Even believers will stand before God in judgment, but our final judgment serves many good purposes, and we ought not to fear it.

REFLECTION & DISCUSSION QUESTIONS

Before the Video

What Do You Think?

Take a moment to answer the following questions. They will prepare you for the lecture.

- Do you fear judgment by God? Why or why not?

- Why do believers still need to stand in judgment before God?

Scripture Reading

Then I saw a great white throne and him who was seated on it. From his presence earth and sky fled away, and no place was found for them. And I saw the dead, great and small, standing before the throne, and books were opened. Then another book was opened, which is the book of life. And the dead were judged by what was written in the books, according to what they had done. And the sea gave up the dead who were in it, Death and Hades gave up the dead who were in them, and they were judged, each one of them, according to what they had done. Then Death and Hades were thrown into the lake of fire. This is the second death, the lake of fire. And if anyone's name was not found written in the book of life, he was thrown into the lake of fire.

—Revelation 20:11–15

- What language indicates that all people will stand before God in judgment? How can this passage be comforting as it relates to death and judgment?

During the Video

Answer the following questions while you watch the video. They will guide you through the lecture.

The Final Judgment and the Gospel *0:00–6:26*

- What is similar about the judgment after death and the final judgment, and what makes them different?

- Why did Paul preach about the realities of the final judgment?

Questions about the Final Judgment *6:26–16:02*

- When is the final judgment? Who will be judging whom?

- What is the standard of God's judgment? Is it the same for everyone?

The Blessed Judgment of Believers *16:02–24:06*

- What must we be careful to stress about our rewards in heaven?

- Will the rewards of others result in our envy in heaven? Why or why not?

After the Video

Answer the following questions after you have finished the lecture. They will help you identify and summarize the major points.

- How is the final judgment related to the gospel?

  If you are in a group, have the members imagine having an opportunity to witness to someone about the truth of the gospel. Ask: Why would it be important to talk about judgment? How would you talk about it? See Acts 24:1–21 for an example of how Paul spoke about the gospel and the final judgment.

- What will happen at the final judgment both for unbelievers and for believers? If you are in a group, have the members read Revelation 20:11–15 again, but this time identifying what is sobering or unsettling about the passage. Ask: What should thinking about the judgment of unbelievers lead us as Christians to do in this life?

- If believers are not to fear final judgment, why should we still reflect on it, and what should the reality of final judgment produce practically in our lives?

  If you are in a group, have the members share their initial reactions to the idea that judgment day can be anticipated and even welcomed by Christians. Ask: As a Christian, have you always thought about judgment day as something like this? What is essential for us to think rightly about judgment?

PRAYER

Commit what you have learned from God's Word in this lesson to prayer.

- Praise God for His just and merciful nature.
- Confess ways that you do not live in light of judgment, spurring you on to put sin to death and do good works in keeping with the faith.
- Thank God that you have been delivered from the final judgment through Jesus Christ.
- Ask God to encourage you with the assurance of the Spirit that there is nothing to fear in judgment so that you might live in eager anticipation for that day.

REVIEW QUIZ

Use these multiple-choice questions to measure what you learned from this lesson.

1. Which of the following was *not* given as an example of Paul's teaching about the final judgment?
   a. Acts 17 on the judgment of all people
   b. Acts 24 on the judgment of all people
   c. Romans 2 on the judgment by Christ
   d. Revelation 20 on the judgment before the throne

2. The reality of judgment, while not itself good news, is essential to the gospel.
   a. True
   b. False

3. When does the final judgment take place?
   a. Upon one's faith in Christ
   b. Immediately after death
   c. Before the resurrection
   d. After the resurrection

4. All people will be judged in accord with all that God has revealed about Himself in Scripture.
   a. True
   b. False

5. What aspect of God's nature was emphasized as a reason that Christians go through the final judgment?
   a. His love
   b. His mercy
   c. His impartiality
   d. His eternality

6. What reason was given for why the Apostles looked forward to the day of judgment without fear?
    a. They had been called by Christ for their work.
    b. They faithfully delivered the teachings of Jesus to others.
    c. They would come before the bar of judgment as already justified.
    d. They would be able to point to their many great works for the kingdom.

Answer Key—What Does the Bible Teach about the Final Judgment?

REFLECTION & DISCUSSION QUESTIONS

Before the Video

What Do You Think?

These are personal questions. The answers should be based on your own knowledge and experience.

Scripture Reading

- What language indicates that all people will stand before God in judgment? How can this passage be comforting as it relates to death and judgment?

  This passage tells us that "the dead, great and small," were standing before the throne of judgment. By that phrase "great and small," we can understand that all people will be called to account in judgment. While the lake of fire may be terrifying, notice that it is "Death and Hades" that are thrown into it. For those who know Christ, whose names are in the book of life, there is no more death but eternal life.

During the Video

The Final Judgment and the Gospel

- What is similar about the judgment after death and the final judgment, and what makes them different?

  What is similar about the judgment after death (see Heb. 9:27) and the final judgment is the verdict, which does not change after we die. God does not change His judgment concerning us before the final judgment. What makes these judgments different, however, is that the final judgment is public, even cosmic, and will not be followed ever again by another judgment.

- Why did Paul preach about the realities of the final judgment?

  The reason that Paul preached the judgment to come was to impress on his hearers the seriousness of his message. The good news of Jesus Christ is sinners' source of relief and mercy in the face of that final judgment. Responding to this gospel in faith is a matter of life and death.

Questions about the Final Judgment

- When is the final judgment? Who will be judging whom?

The final judgment takes place immediately after the bodily resurrection (John 5:28–29). Though we do not know the day or the hour, that day is certain and fixed in the counsel of God. On that day, Jesus Christ Himself will judge the wicked angels and all humanity (see Matt. 25:32; 2 Cor. 5:10; Jude 6).

- What is the standard of God's judgment? Is it the same for everyone?

  The standard of God's judgment is the law of God. People will be judged according to the light that they have received. Those who knew the Word of God will be judged by it, but those who did not have the knowledge of Scripture will be judged according to the moral law that God has revealed to all people. They will be judged according to conscience, which knows what God requires and forbids.

The Blessed Judgment of Believers

- What must we be careful to stress about our rewards in heaven?

  Christians will be rewarded in proportion to their good works. This does not mean, however, that we can import a salvation-by-works-righteousness theology into Scripture's teaching about the final judgment. We are saved by grace alone and are only "unworthy servants" (Luke 17:10), such that even our rewards are entirely gracious.

- Will the rewards of others result in our envy in heaven? Why or why not?

  While some Christians are rewarded more than others, graciously in proportion to and not on the basis of their good works, rewards speak to the different capacities to take in all that heaven is. We serve Christ in this life so that we may enjoy Him as much as we can in the next. But because heaven is a world of perfect love, there will be no envy.

After the Video

- How is the final judgment related to the gospel?

  If left in our sinful and fallen states when we die, we will come before Jesus Christ to be condemned on the day of final judgment. The Judge is the very One who bore the judgment of God on the cross. He paid the penalty for the sins of His people. Everyone who trusts Christ for salvation knows that the sentence of final judgment is rendered for them in Christ. Christians are counted righteous through faith in Him, and this verdict is one that we carry with us all through our Christian life and straight to the bar of judgment. There is no longer any condemnation for us to fear, and there is no possibility that God will annul or reverse our justification in Christ.

- What will happen at the final judgment both for unbelievers and for believers?

  The picture that we are given in Scripture is that on the day of judgment, God will have all manner of people and angels gathered before Him. All people will be sorted out and ultimately ushered into their eternal destinies. While the righteous in Christ will not be condemned, the wicked will be judged in varying degrees for their sins. The verdict that they receive will be just, and it will be acknowledged by them to be just. Believers, likewise, will be gathered but will be set at Christ's right hand and will be openly pronounced "righteous in Christ."

- If believers are not to fear final judgment, why should we still reflect on it, and what should the reality of final judgment produce practically in our lives?

  Believers will face judgment for a number of reasons, many of them practical. Our good works will be put on display, showing forth God's goodness and mercy. This ought to prompt us to pursue good works now. We are also told of the judgment day in Scripture so that we would be watchful over ourselves concerning sin. The reality of judgment also teaches us to let vengeance be the Lord's so that we do not feel the need to seek revenge when we are hurt or persecuted as Christians. Thus, reflecting on judgment stirs us up to holiness and good works, makes us watchful over sin, and enables us to entrust our cause to the Lord.

REVIEW QUIZ

1. **D.**
   The Apostle Paul would heartily affirm the teaching of the final judgment in Revelation 20 as part of God's Holy Word. He did not, however, write the book of Revelation. The places that were pointed to as examples of Paul's teaching on the final judgment were in his speeches in Acts and in Romans 2.

2. **A.**
   The gospel is the answer to the condemnation of judgment. On the cross, Jesus Christ bore the judgment-day penalty of all who believe and trust in Him. The gospel is good news that follows the bad news of certain judgment before a holy God.

3. **D.**
   Hebrews 9:27 teaches that judgment follows death, but that the final judgment happens after the resurrection of the dead. Both the righteous in Christ and the wicked will be raised before facing final judgment.

4. **B.**
   Not everyone is aware of all that God has revealed about Himself in Scripture. Those who perish apart from God's Word, however, will be judged according to conscience, which is a witness to them of God's moral demands, and they will be judged according to this measure of light that they have received.

5. **C.**
   Though Christians will not be condemned on the day of final judgment, a rich expression of God's love and mercy, they will still stand before Him in judgment. Both the righteous in Christ and the wicked will be judged because of God's impartiality, which is taught throughout Scripture.

6. **C.**
   The Apostles did not look forward to the day of judgment to boast in and be acquitted by their good works. They did, however, rest in the good works of Another: Jesus Christ. In Him, they were able to see the day of judgment as something to look forward to, having already been justified.

12

What Does the Bible Teach about Heaven & Hell?

INTRODUCTION

There are two eternal destinies in Scripture: heaven and hell. These two places could not be more different from each other, one being eternal life and the other being eternal death. In this lesson, Dr. Waters explores what Scripture teaches about heaven and hell and why Scripture teaches about these realities. For the Christian, reflecting on both realities—heaven *and* hell—helps us along our pilgrimage in this life, granting us greater faithfulness to God.

LEARNING GOALS

When you have finished this lesson, you should be able to:

- Describe what Scripture teaches about heaven and hell
- Explain the purposes behind Scripture's teaching on heaven and hell

KEY IDEAS

- In heaven, the eternal state is better than the intermediate state, but in hell, the eternal state will be worse than the intermediate state.
- Heaven is a place of embodied rest, marked by utter holiness and joy, chiefly in God Himself.
- Hell is a place of embodied torment, marked by depravity and despair for those unreconciled to God and under His righteous judgment.

REFLECTION & DISCUSSION QUESTIONS

Before the Video

What Do You Think?

Take a moment to answer the following questions. They will prepare you for the lecture.

- Will the new heaven and earth be like or unlike our present creation? In what ways?

- What is the greatest joy of heaven? What is the greatest dread of hell?

Scripture Reading

But the day of the Lord will come like a thief, and then the heavens will pass away with a roar, and the heavenly bodies will be burned up and dissolved, and the earth and the works that are done on it will be exposed. Since all these things are thus to be dissolved, what sort of people ought you to be in lives of holiness and godliness, waiting for and hastening the coming of the day of God, because of which the heavens will be set on fire and dissolved, and the heavenly bodies will melt as they burn! But according to his promise we are waiting for new heavens and a new earth in which righteousness dwells.

—2 Peter 3:10–13

- What will happen to the world as we know it? What will our new world be characterized by? What does this mean for us now?

During the Video

Answer the following questions while you watch the video. They will guide you through the lecture.

What Scripture Teaches about Heaven *0:00–8:18*

- Why is our eternal state in heaven better than the intermediate state?

- How will Jesus transform the church when He returns? What will follow from this in heaven?

- What is the ultimate blessing in heaven?

What Scripture Teaches about Hell *8:18–23:46*

- What feature does hell share in common with heaven?

- What are some differences between heaven and hell?

After the Video

Answer the following questions after you have finished the lecture. They will help you identify and summarize the major points.

- What does it mean that heaven is a "state of rest"? What does it not mean?

  If you are in a group, have the members discuss what they hope will be some similarities in the new heaven and earth with the world as we know it now. Ask: Are there any common themes in your ideas about what you hope to find?

- Have you ever heard hell described as the "absence of God's presence"? How is this not right? What will be different about the believer's experience of God's presence in heaven?

  If you are in a group, have the members read Revelation 21. Ask: What imagery in this chapter can be connected to the description of heaven in this lecture?

- What are some practical reasons behind Scripture's teaching us about hell? What about in regard to heaven?

  If you are in a group, have the members brainstorm about some practical ways of becoming more heavenly-minded so that Scripture's purposes in teaching us about heaven and hell are more fully realized for them.

PRAYER

Commit what you have learned from God's Word in this lesson to prayer.

- Praise God for doing all things for His glory and making Himself our greatest heavenly delight.
- Confess any apathy you might have toward evangelism, even in light of hell, or ask God to make you even more zealous in sharing Christ with unbelievers.
- Thank God for your heavenly hope on your pilgrimage through this world.
- Ask God to continue to give you a Christian life now that resembles more fully what you will be in heaven.

REVIEW QUIZ

Use these multiple-choice questions to measure what you learned from this lesson.

1. In this lecture, "heaven" was differentiated from the "new earth."
   a. True
   b. False

2. What is the chief reason for our joy in heaven?
   a. Embodiment
   b. Holiness
   c. God Himself
   d. Saintly fellowship

3. What is *not* part of our heavenly rest?
   a. Activity
   b. Fulfillment
   c. Idleness
   d. Worship

4. Which of the following is *not* a feature of hell?
   a. Embodiment
   b. God's absence
   c. Total despair
   d. Unrestrained sin

5. Heaven can be understood as a description of what we are, in part, as Christians now.
   a. True
   b. False

6. About which Puritan was it said, "Heaven was in him before he was in heaven"?
   a. Isaac Watts
   b. Richard Baxter
   c. Richard Sibbes
   d. Samuel Rutherford

Answer Key—What Does the Bible Teach about Heaven & Hell?

REFLECTION & DISCUSSION QUESTIONS

Before the Video

What Do You Think?

These are personal questions. The answers should be based on your own knowledge and experience.

Scripture Reading

- What will happen to the world as we know it? What will our new world be characterized by? What does this mean for us now?

  Peter describes the world as we know it now as being burned up and dissolved. Dr. Waters will expound on what this means. Knowing what will happen to this world and the type of world that will replace it does have implications for how we live now. Our future world will be marked by righteousness, and in light of the world that is fading away, Peter calls us now to lives marked by righteousness—"lives of holiness and godliness" (1 Peter 3:11).

During the Video

What Scripture Teaches about Heaven

- Why is our eternal state in heaven better than the intermediate state?

  Paul indicates that the intermediate state when we are with Christ in heaven yet without our resurrection bodies is preferable to life as we know it now. Yet our eternal state in Christ is even better. Then our souls, perfect in holiness, will be reunited with our glorious resurrection bodies. The eternal state is better than the intermediate state in this regard.

- How will Jesus transform the church when He returns? What will follow from this in heaven?

  When Jesus returns, the church will be "without spot or wrinkle or any such thing, . . . holy and without blemish" (Eph. 5:27). Nothing unclean will enter the new Jerusalem; there will be no more sin (see Rev. 21:9–27). With the absence of sin, heaven will be a place of complete joy and happiness.

- What is the ultimate blessing in heaven?

  Heaven is the dwelling place of God (Rev. 21:3), so the deepest reason for our joy in heaven and our ultimate blessing is God Himself. The chief reason for our complete abiding joy is the presence of the living God—Father, Son, and Holy Spirit. We will see and enjoy the triune God and His presence with us in all His goodness forever.

What Scripture Teaches about Hell

- What feature does hell share in common with heaven?

  In our eternal state after the resurrection, heaven is the dwelling place of believers, and we will spend eternity there as body and soul. Hell is likewise a place where people spend an eternity embodied, and just as the eternal state will be better than the intermediate state in heaven, so the eternal embodied state will be worse than the intermediate state in hell.

- What are some differences between heaven and hell?

  Heaven is a place of rest, but Isaiah tells us that "there is no peace . . . for the wicked" (48:22), so there will be no rest from the torments of hell for the wicked. Heaven is marked by love, harmony, and freedom from all sin, but in hell, there will be a society unrestrained in its sin and hatred of God and neighbor. There will thus be no happiness or joy, and God's presence will not be a blessing but a judgment.

After the Video

- What does it mean that heaven is a "state of rest"? What does it not mean?

  In heaven, we can rest from our struggle with sin and temptation, our fighting against the world, the flesh, and the devil. We will also enjoy the Sabbath refreshment of completing the work that God has given us to do in this world. We will find rest in the worship of our God and enjoy God's people. All this means that heaven is not a place of inactivity, sterility, or boredom. Though we will have rest, heaven is an active place that is full of life, free from all corruption or decay as we go from strength to strength.

- Have you ever heard hell described as the "absence of God's presence"? How is this not right? What will be different about the believer's experience of God's presence in heaven?

  We might have often heard it said that heaven is the absence of God's presence, but God is omnipresent and will be present in hell. The worst thing about hell is not that God is absent but that He is very much present in righteous judgment of the unreconciled forever. This is a solemn thing to think about. Believers, however, will have a different experience of God. Our seeing Him will be transformative, and we will be perfectly conformed to Him as His image bearers to dwell in and bask in His delightful presence.

- What are some practical reasons behind Scripture's teaching us about hell? What about in regard to heaven?

The reality of hell teaches us about the evil of sin and the judgment that it deserves, which can help us not to excuse our sin but to see it in the light of God's holy character. Hell impresses on us our need for Jesus Christ, that we must seek refuge in Him by God's grace. Knowing Christ and knowing about the realities of hell should also stir us up to thankfulness, not only for being delivered from hell but for the hell that Jesus Christ experienced on our behalf for our deliverance. Scripture teaches us about heaven to help us in our pilgrimage in this world and toward holiness. If our minds and hearts are filled with thoughts of heaven, then we will be stirred up to serve God on this earth in richer obedience, purifying ourselves as He is pure (1 John 3:3).

REVIEW QUIZ

1. **B.**
   Throughout this lecture, "heaven" has been used as an all-inclusive term to refer to the eternal state, which includes both the new heaven and the new earth. It has been used to refer to our embodied eternal home with God that is lived out in the new heaven and earth.

2. **C.**
   All these will be a true source of joy and happiness in heaven, and we will be blessed because of them. Our chief blessing and source of joy is, however, God Himself. The answer to the first question of the Westminster Shorter Catechism tells us that man's chief end is to glorify and enjoy God forever. Just as He is our chief end now, He is our chief enjoyment forever.

3. **C.**
   Rest in heaven will not be sterile, boring, or idle inactivity. It was stressed that heaven will be a place full of life. Scripture uses the imagery of a feast to describe what heaven will be like. Though it is a place of everlasting rest, it will not be a place of directionless idleness.

4. **B.**
   All these realities will be present in hell, but God will also be very much present in hell. Hell is not the absence of God; God is present in judgment forever against those who are unreconciled to Him in hell.

5. **A.**
   In some sense, we are now what we will be in heaven. We are justified in Christ completely and are being sanctified day by day, such that heaven is not only a destination but a description of what we are now only in part. We live out the Christian life in a deep desire for what we will soon fully be.

6. **C.**
   One of the great encouragements that Scripture's teaching about heaven gives us is that God finishes what He starts and even now is working heavenly qualities in us.

Both Richard Baxter and Richard Sibbes were quoted in this lecture, but it was said of Sibbes that "heaven was in him before he was in heaven."